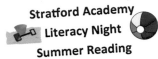

CREATIVE KIDS

The National Parenting Center
Seal of Approval

Science Fair Projects

Helping Your Child Create a Super Science Fair Project

Ages 8–12

Written by Dana M. Barry, Ph.D., C.P.C.

Practice Projects by Robert W. Smith

Illustrations by Howard Chaney

Cover by Denise Bauer

Teacher Created Materials, Inc.

TCM 2600

Teacher Created Materials, Inc.

6421 Industry Way

Westminster, CA 92683

www.teachercreated.com

© 2000 Teacher Created Materials, Inc.
Reprinted, 2002, a

Made in U.S.A.

ISBN #1-57690-600-0

Library of Congress Catalog Card Number: 00-107858

Editor

Walter Kelly, M.A.

Table of Contents

Introduction

Changes and Problems

Our world continues to change. With changes come problems. To live comfortably in such a world, one has to adapt to change by identifying and creatively solving problems. *Science Fair Projects* gives children an opportunity to identify interesting problems and a chance to carry out investigations to solve them. While doing their investigative projects, children build self-esteem and self-confidence, they gain knowledge, and they develop science process and critical thinking skills. These skills and this knowledge will help children to identify and solve daily problems, as well as become more productive and successful individuals in today's changing world.

Skills and Information

Science Fair Projects provides the necessary skills and information needed to successfully prepare children for enjoyable and rewarding science fair experiences. It contains many science project ideas and work sheets designed to give students valuable practice in mastering the steps of a problem-solving model. It also has activities to help children plan, complete, and present their science fair projects with confidence and enthusiasm.

The opening Problem-Solving Model section serves as an excellent guide for teachers, parents, and their children. It describes a problem-solving model in detail and provides a completed science fair project.

Sample Investigations and Inquiry

The final section of *Science Fair Projects* contains five projects adaptable to an inquiry approach that is more open-ended than some conventional science fair projects. These projects, while using the traditional problem-solving model (*Question—Hypothesis—Materials—Variables—Controls—Procedure—Data—Results—Conclusion*), may also be used solely as enjoyable activities leading to further investigation. These activities may all be used to gather data and make observations and conclusions.

Curiosity and Learning

Curiosity, however, will drive interest in the projects, and scientific habits of observation, multiple trials, data gathering, and drawing conclusions will be developed as valuable learning tools. Thus, the true appeal of science—curiosity about the world—will be harnessed to drive a child's love of learning.

The Problem-Solving Model

Teacher Information

This book provides the necessary skills and information needed to prepare students for enjoyable and rewarding science fair experiences. It contains activity sheets designed to give students valuable practice in mastering the steps of a problem-solving model. It also has activities to help children plan, complete, and present their science fair projects with confidence. The Importance of the Problem-Solving Model and the pages following (pages 11–18) serve as a guide for students. They describe a problem-solving model in detail and provide a sample science fair project. The contents of this section can be discussed in class and shared at home with parents.

Do the following things:

1. Notify students and parents about the science fair several months before its scheduled date.

2. Ask parents to be a positive influence by providing support and encouragement to their children for the duration of the project. Send them the page entitled Parent Information (page 10).

3. Enthusiastically inform the students that they are being given a special opportunity to do a project of their own choice—one that can be exciting and lots of fun.

4. Mention that science surrounds them and relates to daily life (sports, sleeping, eating, food, pets, plants, money, etc.). Therefore, they have numerous choices for science fair projects. For specific suggestions, refer to the Ideas for Science Projects section in this book (pages 19–34). Some of these suggestions also include helpful hints. The ideas are grouped into two categories—life science and physical science. Help students adjust their projects to the appropriate grade level of difficulty.

5. Encourage students to consider materials and resources available to them when selecting a science project.

6. Discuss pages 11–18 in class with the students and send a copy home to the parents.

7. Have the students complete the activities relating to the problem-solving model (pages 35–48).

8. Have the students master the science process skills of observing, classifying, and measuring. Refer to the information on pages 56 and 57 and the forms on pages 89–94.

9. Have the students record, analyze, and display data using the math concepts of graphing, averaging, and determining percents and ratios (pages 58–77). Practice activities are provided on pages 95–110.

Teacher Information *(cont.)*

Do the following things: *(cont.)*

10. Provide opportunities for the students to practice writing reports and giving oral presentations.

11. Tell the students to use a science project journal to record all information relating to their project and its investigation. The journal is a dated record of what was done, observed, and thought throughout the investigation and experiments (pages 50–53). Blank science journal project forms are provided for students to use on pages 82–86.

12. Stress the importance of using variables and controls when setting up the experiments. Information can be found on pages 54 and 55. Sample forms are provided on pages 87 and 88.

13. Allow students to practice interpreting data to draw conclusions. Use the information provided on pages 78 and 79 and the samples on pages 111 and 112.

14. Emphasize science safety during experimentation. See pages 8 and 9 for step-by-step information on this important topic. Then notice the student follow-up on pages 80 and 81.

15. Encourage and support each student throughout the duration of the project.

16. Guide students through the process of displaying their projects by using a multimedia approach (pages 113–130).

17. Consider having students carry out some or all of the investigation projects on pages 131–160.

Key Concepts

❑ **Providing Early Notification**

❑ **Providing Support and Encouragement**

❑ **Providing Special Opportunities**

❑ **Relating Science to Daily Life**

❑ **Mastering Science Process Skills**

❑ **Mastering Math Concepts**

❑ **Mastering Recordkeeping**

❑ **Emphasizing Safety**

Teacher Information *(cont.)*

Think Safety First

Following are the eight steps to classroom safety for the science teacher:

1. In class, discuss the importance of science safety.

2. Develop and present to the class a list of safety rules. (See page 9 for a suggested beginning set of safety rules and principles.)

3. Have the students write the safety rules on page 80 of this book.

4. Each student should then enter that list into the beginning of his or her science project journal.

5. Also, it is a good idea to have the students themselves create a poster on which to enlarge the safety rules for display. They should then hang the poster in a prominent place in the classroom.

6. Enforce all safety rules and insist that students follow them when carrying out all science activities and investigations.

7. Supervise all experimental work performed by the students.

8. There can be no more important habit to instill in students than **SAFETY FIRST** in any science environment. It should become second nature to them.

Flow Chart

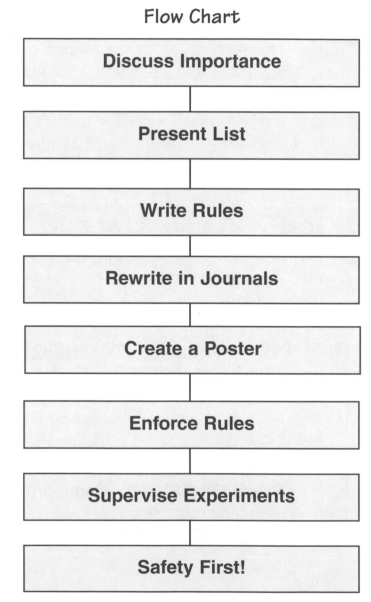

Discuss Importance

Present List

Write Rules

Rewrite in Journals

Create a Poster

Enforce Rules

Supervise Experiments

Safety First!

Teacher Information *(cont.)*

Think Safety First *(cont.)*

Safety Rules

1. Follow all rules that your teacher has for the safe use of animals, chemicals, electricity, etc.

2. Know the location of and how to use all safety equipment like the first-aid kit, the fire alarm, the fire extinguisher, a fire blanket, and eyewash.

3. Before starting any investigation, read all directions and all Material Safety Data Sheets (MSDS) for the chemicals and materials being used. If you have any questions, ask your teacher for assistance.

4. Throughout your experimental work, obtain and wear all of the protective clothing and equipment recommended in the Material Safety Data Sheets. Some protective items include gloves, lab coats, and safety goggles.

5. Get the teacher's approval of your experimental setup and protective attire before you begin.

6. Handle all chemicals and perform experiments under the supervision of an adult.

7. Perform all work cautiously and carefully.

8. Properly dispose of chemicals and do not return unused chemicals to their original containers.

9. Carefully clean up after each science activity.

10. Wash your hands thoroughly after each experiment.

Parent Information

Participation in a school science fair provides exciting and challenging learning experiences for children. It allows them to investigate a problem of interest and to share their enthusiasm and results with others. Children are naturally curious and tend to ask questions like "Why does that work?" and "How does that work?" The science fair project gives children an opportunity to identify an interesting problem and a chance to carry out an investigation and solve it. While doing their investigative projects, children build self-esteem and self-confidence. They gain knowledge, and they develop science process and critical thinking skills. These skills and this knowledge will help them identify and creatively solve daily problems, as well as live more comfortably and successfully in a changing world.

The following helpful and positive actions will be most appreciated by your child and by the teacher:

1. **Encourage** your child to participate in the school's science fair.

2. **Express** interest and provide support to your child throughout the duration of the project.

3. **Offer** to take your child to libraries, computer labs, or other places to obtain information for his or her science project.

4. **Help** your child obtain materials needed for the project.

5. **Read and discuss** pages 11–18 of The Problem-Solving Model with your child.

6. **Emphasize** science safety to your child throughout the investigative project.

7. **Encourage** your child to complete the project on time.

8. **Assist**, if necessary, in transporting the project to and from school. (Have your child write his or her name on all project parts.)

9. **Contact** your child's teacher if you have any questions about the project or the science fair.

10. **Praise** your child for his or her effort and accomplishment at the completion of the project.

Parent + Child + Teacher =

Successful

Science Fair Projects

Importance of the Problem-Solving Model

Over the years, countless schools, museums, and commercial exhibit halls have served in one way or another as the settings for wonderful and sometimes gigantic science fairs. Enthusiastic exhibitors with fantastic and diverse science projects have traditionally attracted people of all ages and from all walks of life.

The displays at these gatherings have usually included oral and written presentations that make use of a range of equipment from the simplest measuring devices to the most complex machines, computers, and electronics. Exhibits have ranged from simple projects with titles like "Paper Airplane Design" or "Chewing Gum Strength" to complex projects with titles like "Earthquake Prediction" or "Rocket Trajectory."

No matter how simple or complex, all of these projects and displays have one purpose in common—to answer a question or solve a problem.

Sometimes these questions are asked by one person, and sometimes they are asked by whole cities or even nations. Why does it rain? How can we predict rain? How can we make it rain? From a child wondering about causes to a nation wanting to improve its crops for food—everyone wants to solve problems. It is human to desire to know and learn things—to solve problems.

Because this has always been true, over time we have developed a model—a regular series of steps—for solving problems. It is also the model we use for almost all projects in science fairs. In fact, it is really a good model to use for solving many problems in life. After all, when you think about it, life itself is really a kind of science fair—a search for the answers to questions. The components, or individual steps, for this problem-solving model will be described in the following pages

Components of the Problem-Solving Model

1 Problem

2 Topic Information

3 Hypothesis

4 Materials

5 Variables

6 Controls

7 Procedure

8 Data Collection

9 Results

10 Conclusion

Components of the Problem-Solving Model

1. Problem

The problem is what needs to be solved. It is the basis for science fair projects. The problem can be defined by posing a question that can be answered by carrying out an experimental investigation. Note the following examples:

- What is the average lung capacity of the students in my class?

- Is a goldfish more active in cold water or warm water?

2. Topic Information

Obtain and record available information that pertains to the topic or problem. Obtain relevant information by reading in the library, watching television, talking to people, and by searching the Internet. One may use these resources to explore the topic of goldfish. Record all information relating to the problem and its investigation in a science journal. This journal is a record of what you did, what you observed, and what you thought throughout your investigation and experiments.

3. Hypothesis

The hypothesis is an educated guess that answers your question. One may guess, for example, that goldfish are more active in cold water than they are in warm water.

4. Materials

Prepare a list of materials needed to carry out the investigation. The goldfish experiment would require materials such as a goldfish bowl, a goldfish, water, ice, a source of heat, and a thermometer.

Components of the Problem-Solving Model *(cont.)*

5. Variables

The variables are those items or conditions that change during an experiment. In the case of the goldfish, the variable is the temperature of the water. It is measured with a thermometer.

6. Controls

Controls are those items or conditions that remain constant throughout the experiment. The controls in the goldfish experiment are the fish, the bowl, and the amount of water.

7. Procedure

The procedure is a set of step-by-step directions to carry out the investigation. It is a method to obtain data to solve the problem. Going through the procedure once is called a trial. At least three trials per investigation are recommended to enhance the accuracy of the data. The values of each trial are added together and divided by three to give an average value for a set of three trial runs.

8. Data Collection

Collect data by making measurements and observations. In the case of the goldfish experiment, water temperature can be measured with a thermometer, and fish activity can be observed at various water temperatures. This information should be recorded in organized charts and tables. (See the ones on pages 14 and 15.)

9. Results

The results of the experiment may be described in words and displayed in graphs, demonstrations, and computer simulations. (Please refer to Displaying Data on pages 68–77 and Displaying the Project on pages 114–130.)

10. Conclusion

A conclusion is an evaluation of the findings of the experiment. It may or may not support the hypothesis.

Components of the Problem-Solving Model *(cont.)*

Goldfish Activity Chart 1

	Date	Warm Water Temperature in Degrees F	Goldfish Activity (none, little, a lot)	Observations
Trial 1				
Trial 2				
Trial 3				
Average				

Components of the Problem-Solving Model *(cont.)*

Goldfish Activity Chart 2

	Date	Cold Water Temperature in Degrees F	Goldfish Activity (none, little, a lot)	Observations
Trial 1				
Trial 2				
Trial 3				
Average				

Components of the Problem-Solving Model *(cont.)*

The following problem and its solution are dedicated to all problem solvers. It is also a good example of a science fair project.

Title: Best Corn Popper

Problem: Which corn popper is the most efficient?

Hypothesis: a microwave or an air corn popper is the most efficient.

Materials: fresh popcorn kernels of any one brand, vegetable oil, measuring cups to measure one-third and one-fourth cups, stopwatch, three large bowls, labels, electric air corn popper, electric corn popper that uses oil, a microwave corn popper

Variable: The variable is the type of corn popper being used.

Controls: The controls in this experiment are the brand of popcorn, the amount of popcorn, and the popper operation time.

Procedure

1. Write the popper types on labels and place a label on each bowl.

Procedure *(cont.)*

2. Measure out one-fourth cup of vegetable oil and place it into the electric popper that uses oil.

3. Measure out one-third cup of popcorn kernels and place the measured kernels into one of the poppers. Repeat this step for each popper.

4. Using a stopwatch, allow each popper to operate for four minutes.

5. For each popper, count the number of kernels that didn't pop. Record this number on a chart.

6. Put each popper's popped corn into the appropriately labeled bowl.

7. Note the appearance of each popper's popcorn. Record the results on a chart.

8. Taste each popper's popcorn. Record the results on a chart.

9. Repeat this procedure two more times to give a total of three trials.

10. Record all data and observations in an organized chart. Remember to write everything that relates to your experimental investigation in your science journal.

Components of the Problem-Solving Model *(cont.)*

Best Corn Popper *(cont.)*

Data Chart

Popper Type	Trial	Popping Time (minutes)	Number of Unpopped Kernels	Popcorn Appearance	Popcorn Taste
Electric Air	Trial 1	4	10	white	plain
	Trial 2	4	15	while	plain
	Trial 3	4	17	white	plain
	Average	4	14	white	plain
Electric with Oil	Trial 1	4	10	white	good
	Trial 2	4	8	white	good
	Trial 3	4	6	white	good
	Average	4	8	white	good
Microwave	Trial 1	4	11	white	plain
	Trial 2	4	12	white	plain
	Trial 3	4	10	white	plain
	Average	4	11	white	plain

Components of the Problem-Solving Model *(cont.)*

Best Corn Popper *(cont.)*

Results

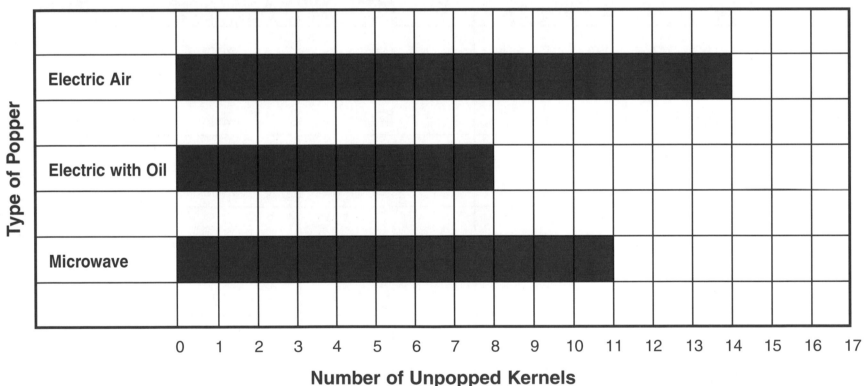

Bar Graph for the Number of Unpopped Kernels

Type of Popper:
- Electric Air — 14
- Electric with Oil — 8
- Microwave — 11

Number of Unpopped Kernels

Conclusion

The most efficient popper for popping the most kernels is the electric popper with oil. It also seems to make popcorn with the best taste. In this investigation, the hypothesis is not supported.

Life Science Projects

Following is a list of life science projects phrased as questions which
can be answered by carrying out experimental investigations.

1. Do ants like sugar better than cheese?	6. Do living plants give off moisture?
2. Do plants grow better in sand or in clay?	7. Does heart rate increase with exercise?
3. Do pea plants grow better with tea or with water?	8. Can objects be identified by the sense of smell?
4. What types of birds come to the schoolyard?	9. Does sound travel better through solids, liquids, or gases?
5. What type of birdseed do birds prefer?	10. Can one produce high-pitched sounds using water?

Life Science Projects *(cont.)*

11. How far away from the source can people detect a sound?

12. How far does a worm travel in five minutes?

13. How does water move in plants? (Hint: Place some celery in a glass of colored water.)

14. Does lung capacity depend on height? (Hint: Have people of different heights blow once into the same type of balloon. Tie each balloon and then measure its circumference.)

15. How long does bread mold take to grow?

16. What conditions are necessary for bread mold to grow?

17. How do observations differ when using the sense of touch versus the sense of sight?

18. What material exchanges take place in an ecosystem? (Hint: Prepare an aquarium with fish, snails, and aquatic plants.)

19. What plant and animal life exist in a 6" x 6" (15 cm x 15 cm) plot? (Hint: Rope off a plot that can be checked each day. Use a magnifying glass and handbooks to identify plant and animal types. Try to estimate the number of each population type.)

Life Science Projects *(cont.)*

20. Can one grow pea plants and produce offspring from them?

21. What things do cows depend on?

22. How much food does a cat eat in a week?

23. Is a goldfish more active in cold or in warm water?

24. Can digestion be simulated? (Hint: Use vinegar to imitate stomach acid. Place food items such as crackers and pretzels into a cup of vinegar and note what happens.)

25. How long does it take for a whole potato to sprout new plants?

26. What are a pet's activities for a week? (Hint: Observe the activities of a pet at different times during the day for a week.)

27. What do ants do on an ant farm? (Hint: Make an ant farm to observe. Collect several ants. Then place them, along with some soil and food scraps, into a transparent jar. Use a rubber band to cover the top of the jar with a piece of cheesecloth.)

28. Are insects more active in warm or in cold environments?

29. How does the growth of a plant provided with sunlight compare to the growth of a plant kept in the dark?

30. How does a spider make a web?

Life Science Projects *(cont.)*

31. Can most people tell the difference between a name brand and a generic soda of the same type?

32. On what part of the tongue do most people sense a salty taste?

33. Can a finger painting be made using vegetables? (Hint: Add beet greens and some water to a microwave dish. To another dish add beets and water. Heat the dishes in the microwave oven for a few minutes and then try some finger painting after the contents have cooled.)

34. On what part of the tongue do most people sense a sweet taste?

35. On what part of the tongue do most people sense a sour taste?

36. On what part of the tongue do most people sense a bitter taste?

37. Does a flower seed grow better by using plain water or by using water with sugar in it?

38. Can you identify a classmate by his or her handprint? (Hint: Make handprints using finger paints and then compare them.)

39. How does outdoor scenery look different through sunglasses?

40. Can a mouse find food in a maze?

Life Science Projects *(cont.)*

41. In my class, who has the longest arms—boys or girls?

42. What is the most frequent eye color in my class?

43. Do plants grow toward sunlight?

44. What type of life is in a drop of pond water?

45. Can the girls in my class jump higher than the boys can?

46. How many calories do I consume in one week?

47. How long can the girls (or boys) in my class hold their breath?

48. What items can be identified by the sense of hearing?

49. Can the boys in my class whistle better than the girls can?

50. What patterns do earthworms make in dirt?

51. What items can be balanced on one's finger?

Physical Science Projects

Following is a list of physical science projects phrased as questions
which can be answered by carrying out experimental investigations.

1. What objects sink in water?	6. What type of juice is the most acidic? (Hint: Test various juices with litmus and pH paper.)
2. What brand of peanut butter spreads over the greatest area?	7. Which paper towel is the strongest?
3. What kind of cereal contains the most iron?	8. Can a mixture of colors be separated? (Hint: Use paper chromatography. Mix two water-soluble colors together. Place a large sample dot of the new color in the middle of a paper napkin strip. Then carefully hold the bottom part of the napkin strip in a cup of water and observe what happens.)
4. What type of bubble gum makes the biggest bubble?	9. How long does it take for one cup of water to evaporate?
5. How far will a piece of gum stretch before it rips apart?	10. How much salt must be added to a glass of water for an egg to float?

Physical Science Projects *(cont.)*

11. Which United States coin has the greatest volume? (Hint: Separately place coins into a graduated cylinder containing water. Determine the coin volume by water displacement.)

16. How much juice does an orange contain?

12. What objects float in water?

17. What is the most acidic fruit? (Hint: Test various fruit juices with litmus and pH paper.)

13. What type of cereal gets soggy first?

18. What objects are attracted to a magnet?

14. What materials dissolve in water?

19. How far can a rubber band be stretched before it breaks?

15. What diaper brand holds the most water?

20. What are some properties of carbon dioxide gas? (Hint: Use safety glasses to prepare carbon dioxide gas by reacting baking soda and vinegar. Attach a balloon containing baking soda to a bottle containing some vinegar. Capture the gas in the balloon and check out its properties.)

Physical Science Projects *(cont.)*

21. Is vegetable oil denser than milk?

22. Is corn syrup more viscous than vegetable oil? (Hint: *Viscous* means a resistance to flow.)

23. Is aluminum foil or cloth a better insulator?

24. Which dish soap makes the largest bubbles?

25. Which dish soap's bubbles last longest?

26. Will water that is exposed to sunlight heat up faster in a white cup or in a colored cup?

27. Which way does the wind blow most frequently in your town?

28. Can information be obtained about unseen objects? (Hint: Place various objects in a shoebox. Seal the box. Then have people examine the box to come up with information about its contents.)

29. Can sand be separated from salt in a mixture?

30. What minerals do rocks contain?

Physical Science Projects *(cont.)*

31. How many inches of rain fall in one month?	36. How do bulbs light up by using batteries?
32. What type of paper is best to make paper airplanes fly a long distance?	37. What are some physical properties of rocks? (Hint: Physical properties include color, size, shape, and mass.)
33. Do paper clips affect the distance a paper airplane flies?	38. Can solar energy be used to cook food? (Hint: Carefully make a solar cooker, using a soda can and a metal rod. Cut away some of the soda can so that the food placed in it will be exposed to the sun. A metal rod may be used to hold the food in place.)
34. To what length can cotton candy or taffy be stretched before it breaks?	39. What type of wing design provides the greatest lift to an airplane?
35. What pencil length has the most stability?	40. What happens if one freezes wet rocks? (Hint: Wet some rocks and then individually seal them in freezer bags before putting them into the freezer.)

Physical Science Projects *(cont.)*

41. What happens to an egg stored in a container of vinegar?

42. How can sound be produced?

43. How many drops of water will balance on a quarter?

44. How many drops of soapy water will balance on a quarter?

45. What are the properties of a burning candle?

46. Can a dirty water sample be filtered?

47. How far can a plastic ball be thrown?

48. Can music be made by using bottles of water?

49. What distance can an egg be dropped before it breaks? (Hint: Design a protective container for the egg before you try dropping it from various heights.)

50. What constellations are found in the sky during the spring?

Physical Science Projects *(cont.)*

51. What size marble will move fastest in vegetable oil?

52. In what brand of shampoo will marbles move the slowest?

53. How much mass can a sheet of paper hold before it rips?

54. What is the average number of seeds in a Valencia orange?

55. Does a small ball roll a greater distance than a large ball?

56. Which cereal type contains the most sugar?

57. How does eliminating half of the butter in a chocolate chip cookie recipe affect the cookie's taste?

58. What is the most efficient corn popper?

59. Can a person make a magnet?

60. Can a drop of water be used as a magnifier?

Physical Science Projects *(cont.)*

61. How does a cooked egg differ from a raw one?

62. How many marshmallows are in a box of cereal containing marshmallows?

63. How do the properties of old pennies compare to the properties of new pennies?

64. How long does it take for a cut apple to oxidize in air? (Hint: *Oxidation* is the browning process.)

65. Does a ball roll the same distance in dirt as it does in grass?

66. Does adding wheels to an object reduce its friction?

67. What type of glue makes the strongest bond?

68. How far can a water balloon be rolled before it bursts?

69. What objects can be lifted by using a lever?

70. What liquids are basic—that is, alkaline? (Hint: Test various liquids using litmus and pH paper.)

Physical Science Projects *(cont.)*

71. How much water must be added to a cup of milk for the milk to lose its color?

72. What items can be smoothed by using sandpaper?

73. What are the properties of water?

74. Do toy cars with big wheels go a longer distance than those with small wheels?

75. How does the length of a vibrating object affect its sound?

76. How much water can a sponge hold?

77. How long will an inflated balloon stay inflated?

78. What ratio of colors exists in a bag of colored, candy-coated chocolate?

79. How long does it take for a container of milk to sour?

80. How much liquid does a Popsicle contain?

Physical Science Projects *(cont.)*

81. How many times can a piece of paper be folded in half?	86. Do liquids cool as they evaporate?
82. How much sugar will dissolve in a cup of water?	87. Which material keeps things colder—plastic wrap or aluminum foil?
83. What type of juice best cleans coins?	88. Does the color of a material affect its heat absorption?
84. Can one make crystals out of sugar and water?	89. At room temperature, does an ice cube melt faster in air or in water?
85. Does temperature affect the amount of sugar that will dissolve in a cup of water?	90. Does water with salt boil faster than plain water?

Physical Science Projects *(cont.)*

91. Is it possible to see and measure a magnetic field?

92. Is it possible to make bubbles of different shapes?

93. How can we determine the hardness of different rocks?

94. What materials will rust?

95. How do crystals of table salt, Epsom salt, and alum differ from one another?

96. How does a thermometer work?

97. Is it possible to map the moon changes for 30 days?

98. How many different ways can we see static electricity at work?

99. Which shape—a sphere, a hoop, or a disk—will roll down a hill the fastest?

100. Is it possible to mix colored light rays to create new colors?

Planning the Project

Getting Started: Introduction

Selecting a Topic

You should do some brainstorming in class to come up with topics and ideas of interest. Write everything on the chalkboard. If more ideas are needed, then visit the school library to look at books and magazines. You may also make use of a computer lab to search the Internet. There are so many interesting areas of knowledge in today's world that everyone should be able to find something he or she would like to know more about.

Brainstorming

Books

Magazines

Internet

Library

Forming the Best Questions

Now that you have ideas, you are ready to ask questions. It is important to think about how you ask questions. The way you ask a question will often determine how it can be answered. Consider, for example, these various approaches or different ways to ask a question.

❏ Some questions can be answered by "yes" or "no."
 Examples: *Did you eat breakfast today?*

 Did you take a shower this morning?

❏ Some questions can be answered by making a choice.
 Examples: *Do you like jelly or peanut butter better?*

 Which color do you like better—red or blue?

❏ Other questions can't be answered "yes" or "no" or by making a choice.
 Examples: *How much taller are boys than girls?*

 How much faster is a car than a bicycle?

Do you see now that how you ask the question will determine how you answer it? This is important in scientific investigations—especially when it comes time to report the results of an experiment.

Getting Started: Introduction *(cont.)*

Forming the Best Questions *(cont.)*

Think about your favorite ideas. What is it that they want to find out about them? Then ask questions about these ideas. You may want to refer to the Ideas for Science Projects section of this book (pages 19–34). Consider what materials and resources are available when forming questions for the science fair projects. Remember that the science project questions should be ones that you can answer on their own by carrying out investigations.

Making a Good Guess (Hypothesis)

Once you have asked the best question for a science project, you are ready to form a hypothesis—a good guess that answers the question. For this step, it is best to learn as much as possible about the topics of their questions so that their answers are smart guesses. You can do research to find information on their topics by reading, talking with knowledgeable people, using past experiences, watching television, and by using the computer to search the Internet.

You are now ready to start research assignments on the topics of their questions. Also, you may wish to select some of the sample science project questions on pages 19–34 and work with others to form a hypothesis for each one. This is good practice before beginning a personal project.

Examples

❑ **Question**: *Which dissolves more completely in water—salt or flour?*

Hypothesis: *Salt will dissolve more completely in water.*

❑ **Question**: *How does the length of a vibrating object affect its sound?*

Hypothesis: *The longer the object is, the lower the pitch will be.*

The following pages (38–48) contain a series of practice sheets to prepare you for carrying out projects in an organized manner.

Getting Started

Selecting a Topic

Below is a list of general topics which may be used to help you think of more specific things they would like to know about.

❏ Mirrors	❏ Sound	❏ Animals	❏ Rockets
❏ Plants	❏ Energy	❏ Birds	❏ Computers
❏ Food	❏ Jets	❏ Toys	❏ Electronics
❏ Money	❏ Weather	❏ Soda	❏ Space
❏ Sports	❏ Cars	❏ Clothes	❏ Health

Getting Started *(cont.)*

Selecting a Topic *(cont.)*

1. Make a list of things that you are interested in and would like to know more about. You may use the list of general topics on the previous page as a starting point, but you are not limited to those ideas.

_____ _____

_____ _____

_____ _____

_____ _____

_____ _____

. . . .

2.   Write your two favorite ideas in the space provided.

_____

_____

Getting Started *(cont.)*

Forming the Best Questions

Below is a favorite idea and questions about it.

Idea: Musical Sounds

Questions

- Does a flute make higher pitched sounds than a tuba?

  (This question can be answered by "yes" or "no.")

- Will thin or thick rubber bands make higher pitched sounds?

  (This question can be answered by making a choice.)

- How are musical sounds produced?

  (This question can't be answered by "yes" or "no" or by making a choice.)

1. Read the following question and write its type in the space provided.

    Question: Can water be used to make musical sounds?

    Question Type:_____

2. Write your favorite idea below.

    Favorite Idea:_____

3. Think about your idea and decide what you want to find out about it. In the space below, tell what you know about your idea and also what more you would like to know.

    _____

    _____

    _____

    _____

    _____

    _____

    _____

    _____

    _____

    _____

    _____

    _____

    _____

    _____

Getting Started *(cont.)*

Forming the Best Questions *(cont.)*

4. Write four questions about your idea. Include a question that can be answered by "yes" or "no," a question that can be answered by making a choice, and a question that can't be answered by "yes" or "no" or by making a choice.

Questions

❏ _____
_____

❏ _____
_____

❏ _____
_____

❏ _____
_____

5. Take a close look at your questions. Decide which one is best for your science project. You want to select a question that can be investigated with materials and resources that are readily available to you. Materials include supplies, and resources include books, magazines, people, computers, etc. Write your best question inside the happy face.

Best Question

Getting Started (cont.)

Forming the Best Questions (cont.)

6. Make a list of materials and resources available to you in the columns provided.

Materials	Resources
_____	_____
_____	_____
_____	_____
_____	_____
_____	_____
_____	_____
_____	_____
_____	_____
_____	_____

• Show your Best Question and lists of Materials and Resources to your teacher for approval.

Getting Started *(cont.)*

Making a Good Guess (Hypothesis)

1. Use your past experiences to write a hypothesis for each question.

    QUESTION: Who can run faster—boys or girls?

    HYPOTHESIS: _____

    QUESTION: How long does it take for a tray of water to form ice cubes after it has been placed in a freezer?

    HYPOTHESIS: _____

2. Write the question for your science project.

    MY QUESTION: _____

    _____

    _____

    • Show your question to your teacher for approval.

Getting Started *(cont.)*

Making a Good Guess (Hypothesis) *(cont.)*

3. Research (find information for) the topic of your science project question. Obtain information by reading, talking to knowledgeable people, using past experiences, watching television, and by using the computer to search the Internet. In the space provided, write a short paragraph about your science project topic.

Science Project Topic

_____

_____

_____

_____

_____

_____

_____

_____

_____

_____

_____

_____

_____

---

4. Now write the hypothesis for your science question.

MY HYPOTHESIS: _____

_____

• Show your hypothesis to your teacher for approval.

Organizing the Investigation: Introduction

Listing Materials Needed to Test the Hypothesis

You are ready to determine the materials needed to carry out your investigation. Write the list on page 47. For practice, do some brainstorming in class to come up with a list of materials needed to make a cheese pizza. Assume that prepared pizza dough is being used. You should have a general list and a detailed one. Possible material lists are shown below.

General List of Materials	**Detailed List of Materials**
• pizza dough	• one package of Rich's™ enriched white bread dough
• margarine	• one stick of Blue Bonnet™ margarine
• pan	• one round pizza pan
• sauce	• one 27.7 ounce (875 mL) bottle of Ragu™ sauce
• spoon	• one tablespoon
• cheese	• one package of American cheese (24 slices)
• cheese shredder	
• pot holder	
• clock	
• oven	

Organizing the Investigation: Introduction *(cont.)*

Preparing a Step-by-Step Procedure

Prepare an organized set of directions to carry out your investigation. As a class activity, develop a step-by-step procedure to make a cheese pizza. You can use the pizza material list generated by the students in the previous activity. Write everything on paper. A possible step-by-step procedure for making a cheese pizza is as follows:

1. Preheat the oven to 350 degrees Farenheit.

2. Using margarine, grease the top surface of the pizza pan.

3. Next, using your hands, cover the top inside surface of the pizza pan with thawed pizza dough. The dough should have a thickness of one-fourth inch (.6 cm) or less.

4. Using a tablespoon, lightly spread enough of the sauce over the top of the pizza dough in the pan so that the dough doesn't show through.

5. Using the cheese shredder, shred cheese over the top of the pizza to a thickness of one-fourth inch (.6 cm) or less.

6. Using a pot holder, carefully place the pan containing the pizza into the hot oven.

7. Bake the pizza for 20 minutes.

8. Using a pot holder, carefully remove the pan containing the pizza from the hot oven.

9. Turn the oven off and remove the pizza from the pan.

10. Allow the pizza to cool a little before tasting it.

Organizing the Investigation

Listing Materials Needed to Test the Hypothesis

In the columns provided, write the materials needed to carry out your investigation.
Please be as specific as possible with each item in your detailed list.

Example

- General List Item: milk
- Detailed List Item: one quart (.9 L) of 2% milk

General List of Materials	Detailed List of Materials

- Show your list of materials to your teacher for approval.

Organizing the Investigation *(cont.)*

Preparing a Step-by-Step Procedure for the Investigation

1. Write your science project hypothesis below.

   HYPOTHESIS: _____

   _____

2. In the space provided, write an organized set of step-by-step directions to test your hypothesis. When writing your procedure, keep in mind that the item being tested varies. Everything else in the investigation is kept constant. (*Example*: In determining the best corn popper, the item that varies is the type of popper. The type of popcorn kernels, the amount of kernels, and the cooking time are kept the same throughout the experiment.)

Procedure

1. _____

2. _____

3. _____

4. _____

5. _____

6. _____

7. _____

8. _____

9. _____

10. _____

• Show your procedure to your teacher for approval.

Developing the Project

Using the Science Project Journal

You will need to use a science project journal. The journal is a dated, written record of everything you do, observe, and think during your science investigations. It starts with the your question and ends when you have found an answer to the question.

The journal contains a number of dated entries. An entry occurs whenever one enters or writes something in the journal. Entries can be informative, experimental, or general.

- An *informative entry* includes the science project question, information about the question's topic, references, and the hypothesis.
- An *experimental entry* includes the activities performed to test the hypothesis and the observations made throughout the investigation.
- A *general entry* includes thoughts, ideas, diagrams, and photos that are related to the investigation.

Again, you should use a science project journal for their experimental investigations. Remember to date each entry. A sample science project journal with entries is presented on pages 51–53. Discuss it in class.

Using the Science Project Journal *(cont.)*

Informative Entry

Date _____

Question

What are the physical properties of table salt?

Topic Information

Table salt is really sodium chloride. It is an ionic compound consisting of cube-shaped crystals. The salt contains the elements sodium and chlorine. Also, it dissolves easily in water. (Some physical properties include *color, size, shape, mass,* and *solubility.*)

References

- Barry, Dana M., "Sodium Chloride," *The Gale Encyclopedia of Science.* Gale Research: MI, 1996; vol. 5.
- Other references include books, people, and Web sites.

Hypothesis

Physical properties of table salt are that it dissolves easily in water and is a colorless-to-white solid.

Using the Science Project Journal *(cont.)*

Experimental Entry

Date _____

Hypothesis

Physical properties of table salt are that it dissolves easily in water and is a colorless-to-white solid.

Activities Performed

1. I used a magnifying glass and a microscope to examine some table salt.

2. I poured 2 cups (500 mL) of tap water into a clear plastic glass.

3. I added one-half teaspoon (2.5 mL) of table salt to the glass of water. Then, stirred the water with the teaspoon.

Observations

1. Pure table salt appeared colorless. It consisted of cube-shaped crystals.

2. The table salt dissolved easily in the water.

Conclusion

My hypothesis was supported.

52

Using the Science Project Journal *(cont.)*

General Entry

Date _____

Thoughts

- ✓ Was the one-half teaspoon (2.5 mL) of table salt measured properly?
- ✓ What exactly is sodium?
- ✓ What is chlorine?
- ✓ How are they put together to make salt?
- ✓ Will twice as much (1 teaspoon [5 mL] of salt) dissolve just as easily? two teaspoons (10 mL)?
- ✓ When (if ever) will it stop dissolving?

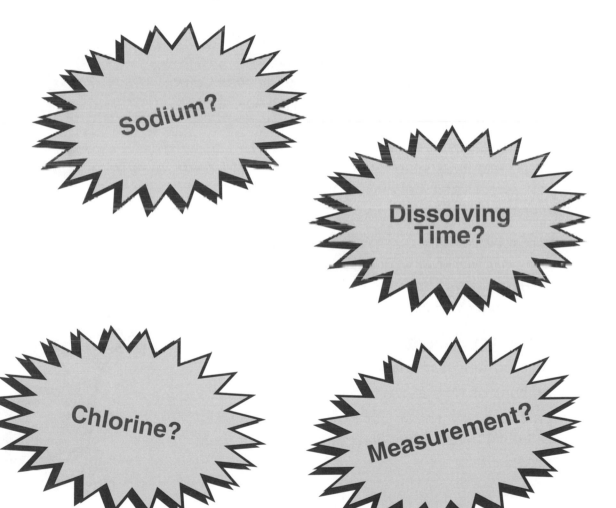

Sodium?

Dissolving Time?

Chlorine?

Measurement?

Setting Up the Experiment

Controls and Variables

It is important to learn about experimental controls, variables, and to study examples of both. A **variable** is the thing or condition that varies or changes as students test a hypothesis, and the things or conditions that stay the same throughout the investigation are the **controls**. Some examples are provided below.

Example 1

Hypothesis: Brand X shampoo produces more foam than brand Y shampoo.

To properly test this hypothesis, the only item that varies is the brand of shampoo (*the variable*). Everything else in the experiment is controlled or kept the same. Controls include the following:

- amount of shampoo used
- amount of water added to each shampoo
- amount of time allowed for foaming to occur
- calibrated container (for example, a graduated cylinder) used to measure the amount of foam produced

54

Setting Up the Experiment *(cont.)*

Controls and Variables *(cont.)*

Example 2

Hypothesis: Pea plants grow faster in a soil consisting of clay than in one consisting of sand.

In this experiment, the variable, or item that changes, is the type of soil (clay or sand). The controls include the following:

- type of pea seed used
- amount of soil used
- type of planting pot
- amount of sunlight provided
- amount of water used

The plants will be checked and measured on a regular basis to compare their growth.

	Day 1	Day 2	Day 3
Clay			
Sand			

Collecting Data

There are several different ways to collect data. The way we decide to collect data usually depends on the type of information that we are seeking, and the type of project or investigation we are doing.

Observing

First of all, we all know that the senses (seeing, hearing, tasting, touching, and smelling) are used in making observations during experimentation. For example, in an experiment where a gas is produced, the following observations might occur:

- Gas bubbles may be seen.
- Gas bubbles may be smelled.
- Gas bubbles may even be heard.

In an experiment designed to find out which part of the tongue detects salt, touching and tasting are very important types of observation to be recorded.

Classifying and Grouping

Many times our data collection involves classifying and grouping similar items together. This method of collecting data helps us to see similarities and differences. For example, in studying the physical properties of rocks, one would group rocks together in the following ways:

- rocks of a similar shape
- rocks of a similar color
- rocks of a similar size

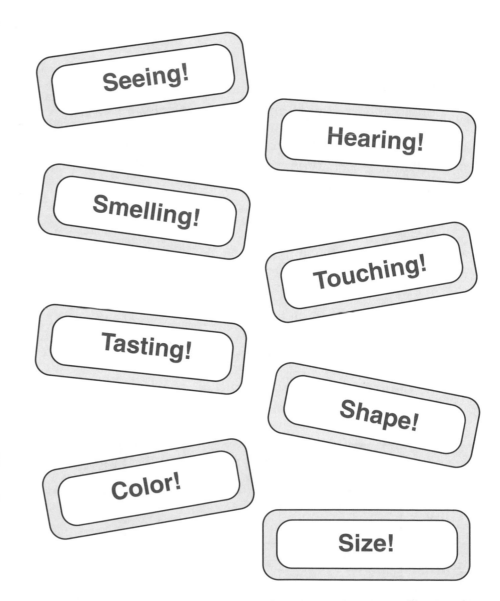

Seeing!

Hearing!

Smelling!

Touching!

Tasting!

Shape!

Color!

Size!

56

Collecting Data *(cont.)*

Measuring

Since all science investigations try to be accurate and exact, the experimental data and information are usually obtained by making measurements. Today, there are many very complicated ways to take measurements, but the following four are basic and very commonly used.

- **Temperature**

  One uses a thermometer to determine the melting point of a chemical.

- **Distance**

  A tape measure can be used to measure the circumference (the distance around something) in inches or centimeters of an inflated balloon.

- **Time**

  The fall time of a marble dropped into a container of shampoo can be measured with a stopwatch.

- **Weight**

  Scales are often used to tell how one object (an apple, for instance) may differ from another in weight or how one object can change over a period of time. There are several different types of scales, some more accurate than others.

Recording Data

As we carry out our investigations, we need to record or write down our data and observations. Charts and tables are very often used for this purpose. **Charts** are used to record data in diverse forms, such as outlines and diagrams. **Tables** are collections of related numbers or items often arranged in parallel columns.

A sample chart and table are shown here and on the next page. Notice that both the chart and the table have titles.

Chart

This chart indicates seed location in a vegetable garden consisting of three rows. The garden is six feet (2 m) wide and 10 feet (3 m) long. A scale is included to provide a realistic view of the garden.

- Corn Seeds (planted four inches/10 cm apart)
- Pumpkin Seeds (planted six inches/15 cm apart)
- Carrot Seeds (planted two inches/5 cm apart)

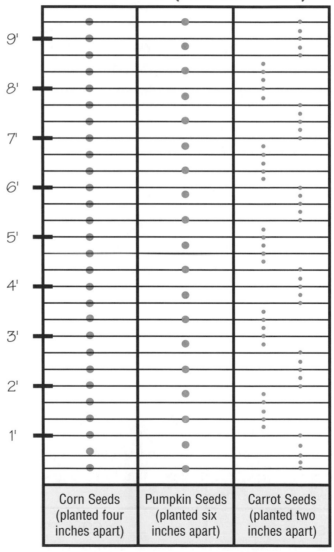

Seed Location in a Vegetable Garden
Scale: 1" = 2' (2.54 cm = .6 m)

Corn Seeds (planted four inches apart)	Pumpkin Seeds (planted six inches apart)	Carrot Seeds (planted two inches apart)

Recording Data *(cont.)*

Table

This table displays the numbers of girls, boys, and teachers who own different pets in a school. Some may own more than one pet.

Elm School Pet Owners and Their Pets

	Number of Girls	Number of Boys	Number of Teachers
Dog	20	18	5
Cat	15	20	4
Parakeet	5	4	2
Canary	0	1	1
Gerbil	6	8	0
Mouse	4	3	0
Snake	2	0	0
Fish	5	5	4
No Pet	12	15	0
Totals	69	74	16

Analyzing Data

As science investigators, you need to analyze your data after recording it. Remember, you may have lots of information to look at. This is because scientific experiments require at least three or more trials to enhance the reliability of the results.

Data for the three (or more) trials can be averaged. Averaging means that we summarize the data into a single measurement, which is considered to be an accurate representation of the results.

Consider the following investigation.

Raisin Cereal Investigation

The average number of raisins in a particular brand of raisin cereal was determined. First, three boxes of the same brand of raisin cereal were purchased. (Keep in mind that at least three trials are run to increase the reliability of the data.) Next, someone counted the number of raisins contained in each of the three cereal boxes.

Box #1 _____

Box #2 _____

Box #3 _____

Analyzing Data *(cont.)*

Raisin Cereal Investigation *(cont.)*

Results

#1   #2   #3

- Cereal box 1 contained 50 raisins.
- Cereal box 2 contained 40 raisins.
- Cereal box 3 contained 45 raisins.

Number of Raisins in Brand X Raisin Cereal

	Trial 1 (Box 1)	Trial 2 (Box 2)	Trial 3 (Box 3)	Average Number of Raisins
Number of Raisins	50	40	45	45

Analyzing Data *(cont.)*

Averages

The word **average** often signifies the usual or typical amount of something. When we are collecting data and using numbers, we try to be exact. There is an exact way to figure out the average for any set of numbers.

The data are averaged into a single measurement. Averages are determined by first adding together the data values of each trial and then dividing the sum by the total number of trials.

In the raisin cereal investigation, for example, one adds the values of 50, 40, and 45 together and then divides the sum of 135 by 3 (*the number of trials*) to get the average value of 45. Based on the data of the given three trials, the average number of raisins per cereal box is 45.

(Notice that an average column is included in the table on page 61.)

Look at the steps taken to compute the average for that table in the space to the right.

Steps to Average the Raisin Cereal Data

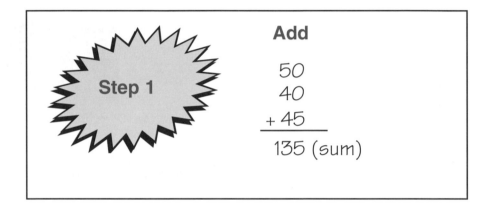

Step 1

Add

$$50$$
$$40$$
$$+\ 45$$
$$135\ \text{(sum)}$$

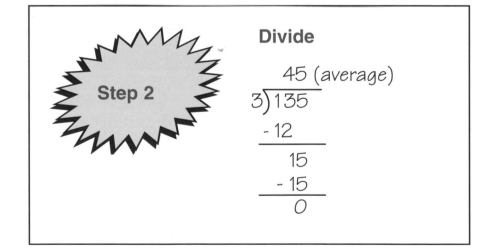

Step 2

Divide

$$45\ \text{(average)}$$
$$3\overline{)135}$$
$$-12$$
$$\overline{15}$$
$$-15$$
$$\overline{0}$$

Analyzing Data *(cont.)*

Ratios

In addition to being expressed in averages, data can also be expressed in ratios. **Ratios** are really just comparisons that make it easy for us to understand exactly how one thing is related to another. For example, if a room contains 20 girls and 10 boys, then the ratio (a comparison) of girls to boys is 20 to 10—or 2:1. This means that there are twice as many girls in the room as there are boys—or for each boy in the room, there are two girls.

If a family includes 3 people with red hair and 9 people with brown hair, then the ratio of people with brown hair to those with red hair is 9 to 3 or 3:1. This means that for every person with red hair, there are three with brown hair.

Ratios are almost always expressed in the smallest possible whole numbers. That is why we would normally say for the example above that the ratio of 9:3 (the exact number of brown-haired persons compared to red-haired persons) is 3:1. Using the smaller numbers lets everybody understand the relationship more easily.

Brown Hair   **Red Hair**

Analyzing Data *(cont.)*

Percents

Data can also be expressed in percents. A whole pie equals 100 percent. Half of the pie equals 50 percent. If a bottle contains 20 marbles, then the number 20 equals 100 percent of the marbles in the bottle. If 10 of the marbles in the bottle are red and 10 of them are blue, then 50 percent (or half of the marbles) are red and 50 percent (or half of the marbles) are blue.

If your students' math background includes percents and decimals, then discuss the following percentage formula with them.

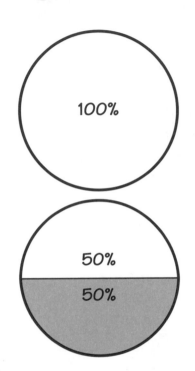

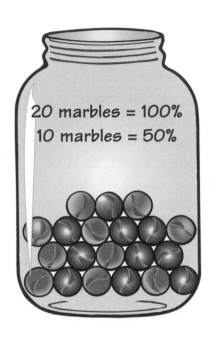

Percentage Formula: % of W = P

Where . . .

% is percent.

of means times or multiply.

W is the whole or total number.

= is equal.

P is the part that we are interested in.

Analyzing Data *(cont.)*

Percents *(cont.)*

- To start, one needs to be able to change a percent to a decimal and a decimal to a percent. To change from a percent to a decimal, the decimal point is moved two places to the left as shown.

> 50% = .50

- To change from a decimal to a percent, the decimal point is moved two places to the right (or the number is multiplied by 100) as shown.

> .75 = 75%

- In words, one can say that the percent (expressed in decimal form) multiplied by the whole equals the part we are interested in.

> % (in decimal form) x W = P
> % x W = P
> 50% or .50 x 20 marbles = 10 marbles

- Also, the part divided by the whole gives us a decimal (which can be changed to a percent).

> P ÷ W = % (in decimal form)
> 10 marbles ÷ 20 marbles = .50 or 50%

- The part divided by the percent in decimal form gives us the whole.

> P ÷ % (in decimal form) = W
> 10 marbles ÷ 50% or .50 = 20 marbles

Analyzing Data *(cont.)*

Percents *(cont.)*

Once we get used to working with percents, it becomes easy. Practice helps us learn to use percents in our thinking and in our science investigations.

Consider the following examples.

Example 1

- If 40% of 25 coins are silver, how many are silver? (Use the percentage formula.)

  % of W = P (Percent times the Whole equals the Part)

  40% x 25 = ?

- Before multiplying, change the percent to a decimal as shown.

  40%   =   .40

$$
\begin{array}{r}
25 \\
\times\,.40 \\
\hline
00 \\
+\,1000 \\
\hline
10.00
\end{array}
$$

- The number of silver coins is 10.

25 Coins

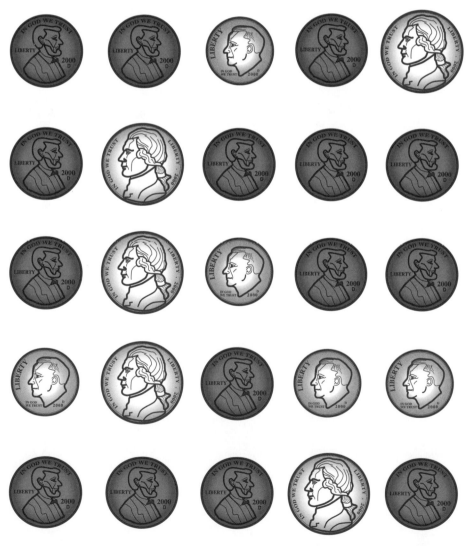

Analyzing Data *(cont.)*

Percents *(cont.)*

Example 2

- The number of students in a class is 40. If 10 of the students are girls, what percent of the students in the class are girls? (Use the percentage formula.)

$$P \div W = \%$$

$$10 \div 40 = \%$$

- The part is divided by the whole. The resulting decimal is multiplied by 100 to obtain the percent of students in the class who are girls. The answer is 25%.

$$\begin{array}{r} .25 \\ 40\overline{)10.00} \\ -80 \\ \hline 200 \\ -200 \\ \hline 0 \end{array}$$

$$.25 \times 100 = 25\%$$

Displaying Data: Results

After data has been collected and organized in a table, it can be displayed in graphs. Since graphs are like pictures, they make it easy for people to see the results of science investigations. Line graphs, bar graphs, and circle graphs are the most commonly used types of graphs. Everyone should be able to read and make each type.

On this page are some typical views of the basic graphs. Explanations and sample graphs with data are provided on pages 69–77. Try drawing each type on the chalkboard and discuss all of them in class. (Some graphs contain individual data values, and others contain averaged data values.)

Typical Bar Graph (two views)

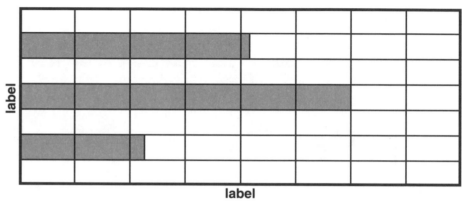

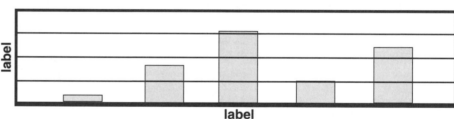

Typical Line Graph

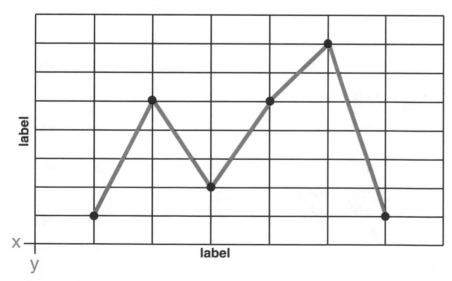

Typical Circle Graph
(sometimes called a "pie chart")

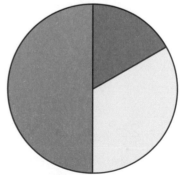

Displaying Data: Results *(cont.)*

Line Graph

A **line graph** is used to show how one or more things changed over a period of time. The line graph is a grid made up of an **x-axis** (horizontal line that goes across) and a **y-axis** (vertical line that goes up and down).

Each axis on the line graph has a label to identify what it represents. The vertical **y-axis** label usually tells what is being measured (for example: color, height, temperature, number of items, etc.). The horizontal **x-axis** label usually tells when the measurements are taken (for example: intervals of seconds, minutes, hours, days, or weeks).

For each fact in a data table, we can place a dot at a particular point on the grid. Each data point (dot) on the grid represents an individual value of collected data or an averaged value of collected data. Lines connecting the data points provide estimated measurements between the points. If more than one line is used to display the data, then each line should be a different color or different design (for example—solids, dots, dashes, etc.) to make comparisons easier.

In addition to horizontal and vertical labels, each line graph should have a title and a key to identify the lines of connected data points.

The sample science project described on this page will become the basis for the data table and line graph that appear on pages 70 and 71.

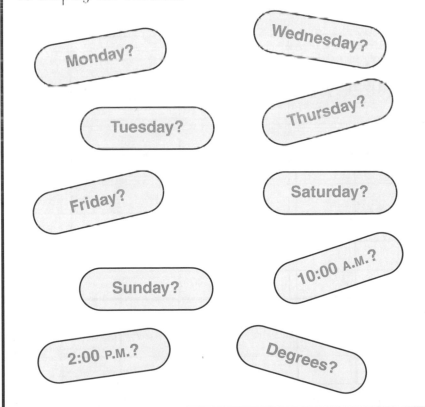

Sue's Science Project

Sue's science project question was "*How does the morning temperature (10:00 A.M.) compare to the afternoon temperature (2:00 P.M.) at my school for a week in November?*" Sue collected data for a week, recorded it in a table, and then prepared a line graph to display her results.

Monday?

Wednesday?

Tuesday?

Thursday?

Friday?

Saturday?

Sunday?

10:00 A.M.?

2:00 P.M.?

Degrees?

Displaying Data: Results *(cont.)*

Data Table

Table of Morning and Afternoon Temperatures at Elm School During a Week in November

		Monday (M)	Tuesday (T)	Wednesday (W)	Thursday (Th)	Friday (F)	Saturday (Sat)	Sunday (Sun)
Temperature in °F	**Morning (10:00 A.M.)**	20°	25°	20°	30°	40°	45°	25°
	Afternoon (2:00 P.M.)	35°	45°	30°	35°	50°	50°	35°

Note: The data from this table can also be seen in the line graph on page 71.

Displaying Data: Results *(cont.)*

Line Graph

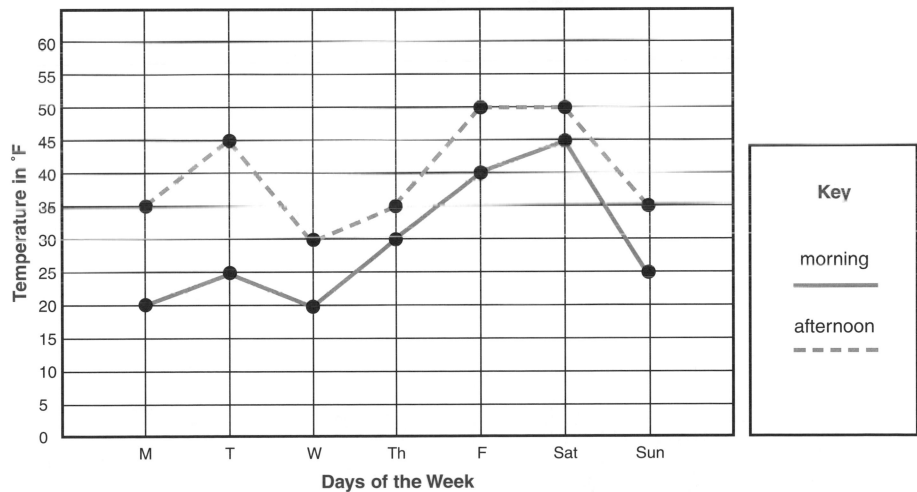

Line Graph of Morning and Afternoon Temperatures at Elm School During a Week in November

Displaying Data: Results *(cont.)*

Bar Graph

A **bar graph** is used to show how totals compare in things such as **distance**, **length**, and **time**. It is drawn on a grid, and the bars may go vertically or horizontally. The labels on the side and bottom of the graph tell what is being compared and the amount of each item. Sometimes bars are grouped together. These bars should be distinguished from one another by color or design to make comparisons easier. In addition to labels, each bar graph should have a title and a key to identify what each bar stands for.

Bars Grouped Together

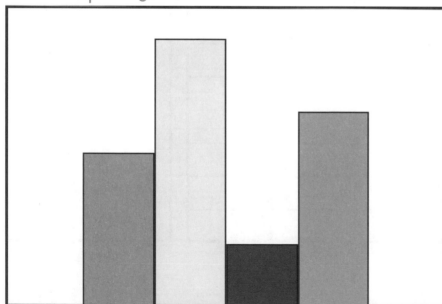

Bars Separated

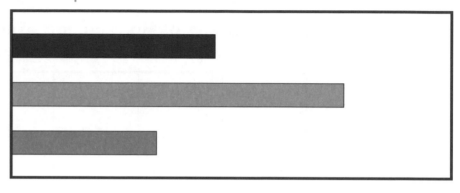

Tom's Science Project

Tom's science project question was "Who eats the most bread for lunch and supper at my house—Tom, Joe, or Linda?" He collected data for four days, averaged it, recorded it in a table, and then prepared a bar graph to display his results.

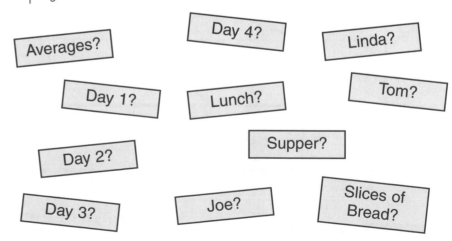

Displaying Data: Results *(cont.)*

Data Table

Table of Bread Consumed for Lunch and Supper at Tom's House

		Day 1 (Trial 1)	Day 2 (Trial 2)	Day 3 (Trial 3)	Day 4 (Trial 4)	Average
Tom	Lunch	4	4	2	2	3
	Supper	4	1	4	3	3
Joe	Lunch	5	4	6	5	5
	Supper	3	4	3	2	3
Linda	Lunch	2	2	2	2	2
	Supper	0	2	1	1	1

Key: Numbers represent slices of bread consumed at each meal.

Note: Data from this data table is also illustrated in the bar graph on page 74.

Displaying Data: Results *(cont.)*

Bar Graph

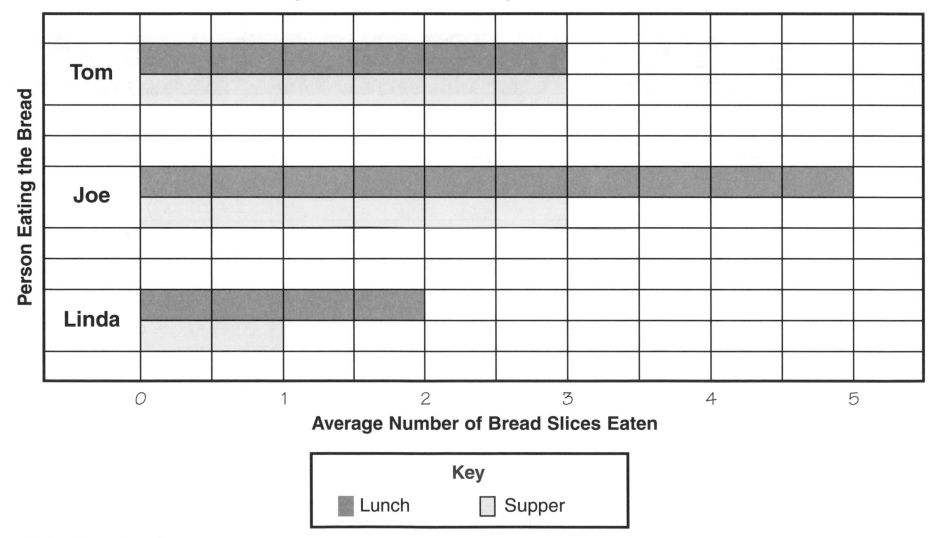

Bar Graph of Bread Consumption at Tom's House

(Y-axis: Person Eating the Bread — Tom, Joe, Linda)

(X-axis: Average Number of Bread Slices Eaten — 0, 1, 2, 3, 4, 5)

Key

■ Lunch   □ Supper

Displaying Data: Results *(cont.)*

Circle Graph

A **circle graph** is used to show the parts of the whole. It will usually be expressed in fractions or percents. This type of graph also includes a title and labels.

To make this type of graph, one must learn to divide a circle into fractions or percents. In addition to a ruler, we use a compass and protractor to do this. Since the total number of degrees in any circle is 360, one simply uses the percentage formula (pages 64–67) to determine how to divide the circle.

Suppose we need to show that Joe ate 50% of a pie, Tom ate 20% of the pie, and Linda ate 25% of the pie.

First, we use a compass to draw a circle. Then we just multiply .50 x 360°. The answer is 180°. Starting at any point on the outside line (circumference) of the circle, we use the protractor to measure and mark off 180° of the circle. We then connect those two points to the center dot of the circle. That part would then be labeled "Joe." Next, to show 20% as another part, we just multiply .20 x 360°. The answer is 72°, so we use the protractor to measure another 72° of the circle and label that section "Tom." Finally, we multiply .25 x 360° (90°) and use the protractor to mark off that portion and label it "Linda." There will be 5% of the circle left, so we label it "Leftover."

Mary's Science Project

Mary's science project question was *"What is the favorite color of the students in the fifth-grade class?"* Out of 100 children in the fifth grade at Elm School, she found that 50 favored the color blue, 25 favored red, 20 favored green, and 5 favored yellow. Mary recorded her data in a table and used a circle graph to display the results.

100 total students?

Blue?   Red?

Green?   Yellow?

$\dfrac{50}{100}$ = _____ % of 360?

$\dfrac{25}{100}$ = _____ % of 360?

$\dfrac{20}{100}$ = _____ % of 360?

$\dfrac{5}{100}$ = _____ % of 360?

Answers: 50%, 25%, 20%, 5%

Displaying Data: Results (cont.)

Data Table

Table of Favorite Colors in the Fifth-Grade Class

Color	Blue	Red	Green	Yellow	Totals
Number of Students	50	25	20	5	100
Fraction	$\frac{1}{2}$ class	$\frac{1}{4}$ class	$\frac{1}{5}$ class	$\frac{1}{20}$ class	1 whole class
Percent (%)	50%	25%	20%	5%	100%

Note: The information in this data table is also illustrated in the circle graph on page 77.

Displaying Data: Results *(cont.)*

Circle Graph

Fifth-Grade Students' Favorite Colors

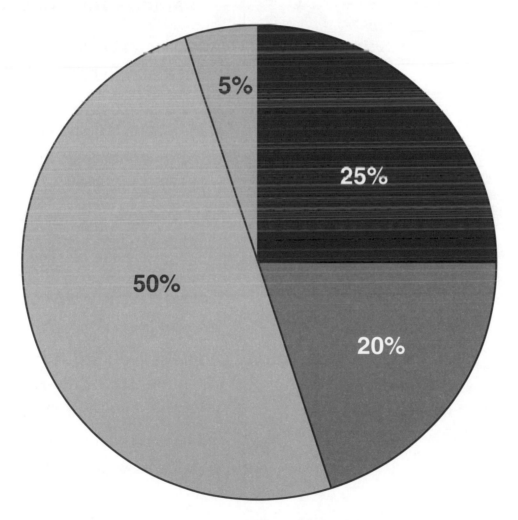

Interpreting Data to Draw a Conclusion

Completing the Project

Remember that when your project is over, you will have carried out the steps of a problem-solving model. You will have a right to be proud of your efforts because everybody who completes a science project learns and makes accomplishments. You are a successful investigator if you are conscientious and do your best.

Interpreting the Project

It is important to remember that after you have completed your investigations, you need to interpret the data in order to draw your conclusions. The conclusion tells the outcome of the project, and that conclusion may or may not support the hypothesis.

Revising t he Hypothesis

Keep in mind that the hypothesis is an educated guess and that you have carried out an investigation to test it. If your experimental data does not support the hypothesis, you should revise the hypothesis in the conclusion statement so that it matches the results. Always remember that finding out that a hypothesis is not supported is just as important as finding out that the hypothesis is supported. Important science discoveries have been made as a result of an unsupported initial hypothesis.

The Story of a Famous Unsupported Hypothesis

Aristotle, an early Greek philosopher, once formed a hypothesis that if two weights were dropped from the same height, the one that was heavier would fall faster and strike the ground sooner than the one that was lighter. It seemed like a logical idea. However, he did not carry out an investigation to check his hypothesis. He just assumed it was true. Many years later, another great thinker named Galileo did carry out such an investigation and learned that Aristotle's hypothesis was not supported. In fact, the different weights would strike the ground at exactly the same time. Thus, an important discovery about Earth's gravity was made—by learning that an early hypothesis was wrong!

Interpreting Data to Draw a Conclusion *(cont.)*

Aristotle's Assumption
(Hypothesis)

If two weights are dropped from the same height at the same time,

Galileo's Investigation
(Testing Aristotle's Hypothesis)

the heavier weight will strike the ground before the lighter weight.

Observation: Both weights strike the ground at the same time.

Conclusion: Aristotle's hypothesis is not supported.

Safety First

Keep safety in mind when carrying out all science activities. In the space provided, write your teacher's special safety rules.

Safety Rules

1. _____
_____

2. _____
_____

3. _____
_____

4. _____
_____

5. _____
_____

6. _____
_____

7. _____
_____

8. _____
_____

9. _____
_____

10. _____
_____

Safety First *(cont.)*

Write a few safety rules of your own. Add an illustration or drawing to show why your rules are important.

My Safety Rules   **Illustration**

1. _____

   _____

2. _____

   _____

3. _____

   _____

4. _____

   _____

5. _____

   _____

Science Project Journal

Keep a dated, written record of your scientific investigation in this journal. (You may use this page and the following four pages as models to duplicate and use in your own journal whenever you undertake a new project.)

Informative Entry

Date _____

Question

Topic Information

_____   _____

_____   _____

_____   _____

_____   _____

_____   _____

_____   _____

_____   _____

Science Project Journal *(cont.)*

Informative Entry *(cont.)*

References

1. _____

2. _____

3. _____

4. _____

5. _____

6. _____

7. _____

8. _____

9. _____

10. _____

Hypothesis

_____

_____

Science Project Journal *(cont.)*

Experimental Entry

Date _____

Activities Performed

1. _____

2. _____

3. _____

4. _____

5. _____

6. _____

7. _____

8. _____

9. _____

10. _____

Science Project Journal *(cont.)*

Experimental Entry *(cont.)*

Observations

1. _____

2. _____

3. _____

4. _____

5. _____

6. _____

7. _____

8. _____

9. _____

10. _____

Science Project Journal *(cont.)*

General Entry

Date _____

Thoughts

_____

_____

_____

_____

_____

_____

_____

_____

Picture

Setting Up the Experiment: Controls

Controls are the items that stay the same throughout an experiment.

Read the following sample hypothesis. Then in the space provided, list the controls necessary to properly test it.

Hypothesis

A ball rolls a longer distance on grass than it does on dirt.

Controls

_____

_____

_____

_____

_____

My Science Project:_____

_____

_____

_____

Hypothesis

_____

_____

Controls

_____

_____

_____

Setting Up the Experiment: Variables

Variables are the items that vary or change during an experiment.

Read the following sample hypothesis. Then in the space provided, describe the variables necessary to properly test it.

Hypothesis

Aluminum metal conducts heat better than copper metal.

Variables

_____

_____

_____

_____

_____

_____

My Science Project:_____

_____

_____

_____

Hypothesis

_____

_____

_____

_____

Variables

_____

_____

_____

Collecting Data: Observing

Observations are made by using the senses of touching, seeing, tasting, smelling, and hearing. Our senses provide us with experimental data as well as information about our surroundings. Consider carrying out an investigation to compare various brands of popped corn. In the spaces provided below and on the next page, describe what you expect to observe by using the five senses.

Hearing

_____

_____

_____

_____

_____

_____

_____

_____

Smelling

_____

_____

_____

_____

_____

_____

_____

_____

Collecting Data: Observing *(cont.)*

In the spaces below, continue describing what you expect to observe in an investigation to compare various brands of popped corn.

Touching

_____

_____

_____

_____

_____

_____

Seeing

_____

_____

_____

_____

_____

Tasting

_____

_____

_____

Collecting Data: Classifying and Grouping

Experimental work includes **classifying**—that is, the grouping of similar items together. For a study relating fruits to color, one would put red-colored fruits such as apples, cherries, and strawberries into a group called Red Fruits. Lemons and bananas would be put into the group called Yellow Fruits. In other words, we would be classifying the fruits by color.

Read over the following investigative descriptions. Then in the spaces provided, list all possible group titles (classifications) for each one.

1. Determine the hair color assortment and number of each type in your class.

Group Titles

_____

_____

_____

_____

Collecting Data: Classifying and Grouping *(cont.)*

Continue listing all possible group titles (classifications) for the following investigative descriptions.

2. Determine the number of boys versus girls in the class who are over five feet tall.

Group Titles

_____

_____

_____

_____

_____

_____

_____

3. Determine whether green grapes have more seeds than purple grapes.

Group Titles

_____

_____

_____

_____

_____

_____

_____

Collecting Data: Measuring

Experimental data and information are obtained by making **measurements**. Measurements include such things as the following:

- timing a race or a reaction
- finding the length of a stretched piece of candy
- figuring out how much matter (solid, liquid, or gas) is in a container
- determining the temperature at which a liquid boils

In the spaces provided, describe completely the types of measurements needed and steps necessary to obtain data for the following investigation.

1. Determine the distance a piece of chewed gum will stretch.

Measurement Description and Steps

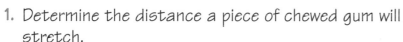

_____

_____

_____

_____

_____

_____

_____

_____

_____

_____

_____

Collecting Data: Measuring *(cont.)*

In the spaces provided, continue describing completely the types of measurements needed and steps necessary to obtain data for the following investigations.

2. Determine if boys can run the 50-yard dash faster than girls can.

Measurement Description and Steps

_____

_____

_____

_____

_____

_____

3. Determine the amount of water that a diaper holds.

Measurement Description and Steps

_____

_____

_____

_____

_____

_____

_____

Recording Data: Charts

When carrying out science investigations, one needs to record (write down) data and observations. **Charts** can be used to record data in such diverse forms as outlines and diagrams. Notice the sample chart below with a title, scale, and labels. This is for a science investigation to determine which type of corn grows fastest in a farmer's home garden.

Chart Title: **Corn Garden Layout**

Multicolored Harvest Corn	
White Popcorn	
Hybrid A Sweet Corn	
Hybrid B Sweet Corn	

Scale: 1 cm = 1 ft.

Recording Data: Charts *(cont.)*

Draw a chart indicating the location of five individual seed types in a flower garden that is five feet (1.5 m) wide and ten feet (3 m) long. Please provide a title, a scale, and labels for your chart.

Chart Title:_____

Scale: _____

Recording Data: Tables

Most experimental data and observations are recorded in **tables**. Tables are collections of related numbers and items, often arranged in parallel columns. The following sample table shows how many students at school X exercise at least one hour each day in one of a selected group of sports. You may use it as a guide for constructing your own table in the assignment on page 98.

Table Title: **Daily Exercise Patterns at School X**

	Skateboarding	Ice Skating	Bicycling	Roller Blading	Soccer
Boys	20	5	15	10	20
Girls	10	20	20	7	13
Total	30	25	35	17	33

Recording Data: Tables *(cont.)*

Read the following study. Then prepare a table for its data. Include a title and labels. Finally, record the data in your table.

Hair Study

A study was carried out to determine the number of students in a class with red, blonde, black, and brown hair. The results are as follows:

- One student has red hair.
- Three students have blonde hair.
- Two students have black hair.
- Seven students have brown hair.

Table Title:_____

Analyzing Data: Averages

Data can be **averaged**. Averaging summarizes the data into a single measurement, which is considered to be an accurate representation of the results. Averages are determined by first adding together the data values and then dividing the sum by the number of values. For example, the average value for the three numbers 10, 12, and 14 is 12. Add the numbers together and divide their sum of 36 by 3 to get the average value of 12.

Add	Divide

```
  Add              Divide

   10               1 2
   12            3 ) 36
  +14              - 3
  ———              ———
   36                6
                   - 6
                   ———
                     0

        Average = 12
```

Determine average values for the data given in the situations on the right side of this page. Do your work on a separate paper.

1. John received test grades of 70, 80, 75, 90, and 90 during the five-week marking period at school. What was his test average for the school's five-week report?

2. Eight girls on the school soccer team have the following weights: 100 pounds, 120 pounds, 85 pounds, 80 pounds, 130 pounds, 97 pounds, 98 pounds, and 130 pounds. What is the average weight?

To find the average, add the numbers together and divide the sum by how many numbers you added.

Analyzing Data: Averages *(cont.)*

Continue determining the average values for the data given in the following situations. Do your work on a separate sheet of paper.

3. Five boys training for an ice skating exhibition spent the following numbers of hours practicing:

   - Fred—3 hours
   - Jim—4 hours
   - Charles—2 hours
   - Ed—5 hours
   - Joe—6 hours

   What was the average number of hours spent on the ice?

4. Although all of them wore helmets and protective pads, six of the girls who regularly skateboarded during a three-month period had falls that required treatment. Jill had 3 falls, Jane had 5 falls, Mary had 6, Betty had 2, and the other two girls each had 1 fall. What was the average number of falls needing treatment during that three-month period?

5. Seven girls in the fifth grade class grew taller than any of the others during the school year. One of them grew 5 inches, two of them grew 3 inches each, two more grew 3.5 inches each, one grew 4 inches, and the last one grew 6 inches! What was the average growth of the seven girls?

6. The temperature inside an ice skating rink must not be allowed to get high enough for the ice to melt—especially when there are many people using the rink. During one especially busy week, the following high temperatures were recorded:

   - Monday—22° F
   - Tuesday—28° F
   - Wednesday—30° F
   - Thursday—25° F
   - Friday—20° F
   - Saturday—19° F
   - Sunday—The rink was closed.

   What was the average temperature for the rink during this week?

Answers: 1. 81, 2. 105, 3. 4, 4. 3, 5. 4, 6. 24

Analyzing Data: Ratios

Data can be expressed in **ratios,** a form of simple whole number comparisons. Consider a boy who has 10 dress shirts that are white in color and one that is blue. A comparison can be made between the number of white and blue dress shirts. The ratio is ten to one or 10:1. This means that for every 10 dress shirts that are white, there is 1 dress shirt that is blue. If the same boy had 20 white dress shirts and 2 blue dress shirts, the ratio would still remain 10:1. That is because ratios are expressed in the simplest whole numbers possible (20:2 is the same as 10:1).

30:3 = 10:1

40:4 = 10:1

50:5 = 10:1

60:6 = 10:1

70:7 = 10:1

_____ = 10:1

Determine ratios for the information provided in the following studies.

1. A grandmother made 5 cherry pies and 1 blackberry pie. What is the ratio of cherry pies to blackberry pies?

Cherry:

Blackberry:

Ratio = _____

2. A family has 4 sons and 2 daughters. What is the ratio of sons to daughters? (Be sure to use the simplest whole numbers possible to express this ratio.)

Sons: X X X X

Daughters:

Ratio = _____

Analyzing Data: Ratios *(cont.)*

Examine the data table below and use the information to report the ratios in the questions that follow.

Number of Students and Teachers at School X Who Own One of the Listed Pets

	Dog	Cat	Bird	Snake
Girls	8	6	2	1
Boys	10	2	1	3
Teachers	2	2	1	0
Total	20	10	4	4

1. What is the ratio of girl dog-owners to boy dog-owners?

   Ratio = _____

2. What is the ratio of boy snake-owners to girl snake-owners?

   Ratio = _____

3. What is the ratio of total bird owners to total snake owners?

   Ratio = _____

4. What is the ratio of girl cat-owners to boy cat-owners?

   Ratio = _____

5. What is the ratio of total dog owners to total cat owners?

   Ratio = _____

Answers: 1. 4:5, 2. 3:1, 3. 1:1, 4. 3:1, 5. 2:1

102

Analyzing Data: Percents

Data can also be expressed in **percent** (%). A whole pie or the whole of any item is considered to be 100% of the item. Frequently used percents and their equivalents are listed in the table below.

Percents and Their Equivalents

Percent	Fraction	Number Out of 100 (total number)
100%	1	100
80%	$\frac{4}{5}$	80
75%	$\frac{3}{4}$	75
50%	$\frac{1}{2}$	50
25%	$\frac{1}{4}$	25
20%	$\frac{1}{5}$	20
10%	$\frac{1}{10}$	10

Determine the percents for the following problems. (Refer to the table for assistance.)

1. What percent of a pie remains if one-fourth of it is missing?

   Percent _____

2. A gumball machine contains 100 gumballs. If 90 are removed, what percent of the gumballs remain in the machine?

   Percent _____

3. If one-fifth of a class went swimming, what percent of the class went swimming?

   Percent _____

4. What percent of that same class did not go swimming?

   Percent _____

Answers: 1. 75%, 2. 10%, 3. 20%, 4. 80%

Analyzing Data: Percents *(cont.)*

Use the Percents and Their Equivalents table on page 103 to help you determine the percents for the following examples.

1. If one-half of the class owned dogs, what percent did not own dogs?

   Percent_____

2. What percent of the class did not own snakes if only one-tenth of them did?

   Percent_____

3. Four-fifths of the science class finished their science fair projects a week early. The remainder finished exactly on time. What percent finished exactly on time?

   Percent_____

   What percent finished early?

   Percent_____

4. Twenty-five out of 100 pet owners prefer cats to dogs. What percent prefer cats to dogs?

   Percent_____

5. If you ate three-fourths of the ice cream in the container, what percent would remain?

   Percent_____

6. Sixty out of 100 gumballs were colored red. Thirty were colored yellow. The remainder were colored blue. What percent were blue?

   Percent_____

7. John bought all the gumballs (100) in the machine. What percent of the gumballs were left after he finished chewing all the yellow ones?

   Percent_____

8. John gave half the red gumballs to his friends. What percent did he have left after chewing all the yellow ones and giving away half the red ones?

   Percent_____

Answers: 1. 50%, 2. 90%, 3. 20%, 80%, 4. 25%, 5. 25%, 6. 10%, 7. 70%, 8. 40%

Displaying Data: Line Graph

This project asks you to display your data in a **line graph**.

A class of 20 students (with an equal number of girls and boys) was given a science test on mass and weight. The girls' science test scores are compared to the boys' scores.

Girls were given numbers from 1 to 10, and boys were also given numbers from 1 to 10. Then the score for girl #1 was compared to the score for boy #1, the score for girl #2 with the score for boy #2, etc.

Use the information from the data table on this page to complete a line graph for this project on page 106. Be sure to include a title and labels for your line graph. After plotting the data points, remember to connect them.

Data Table: Girls' and Boys' Science Test Scores

Student Number	Scores in Percent (%)	
	Girls	Boys
1	70	80
2	80	60
3	90	70
4	90	80
5	100	95
6	100	95
7	60	75
8	50	45
9	80	60
10	90	100

Displaying Data: Line Graph *(cont.)*

A line graph like the one below can be used to display the information from a data table. Use the information from the data on page 105 to complete this line graph.

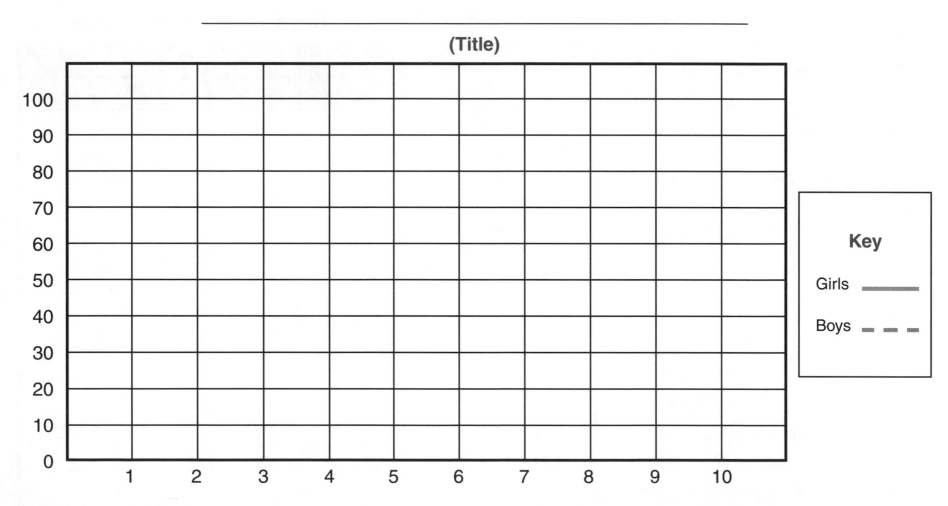

(Title)

Key

Girls ———

Boys – – – –

Refer to your graph to answer the following question. How many times do the boys' and girls' lines intersect (cross each other)? If your answer is 4, you are correct!

Displaying Data: Bar Graph

This project involves dropping a playing marble into containers (all the same size) of various brands of shampoos. In each case, the fall is timed to determine how long it takes for the marble to reach the bottom of each container. The times are then recorded in a data table. The results should tell us which shampoo is the thickest (or most viscous). Several trials are done for each brand of shampoo.

Look over the following data table. Determine the average trial value for each brand of shampoo. Record these values in the table.

After completing this data table, turn to page 108 to complete a bar graph, displaying the data in another manner.

Data Table

Marble Fall Times in Various Brands of Shampoo

Shampoo Brand	Time in Seconds			
	Trial 1	Trial 2	Trial 3	Average Value
A	4	3	5	
B	2	2	2	
C	4	5	6	

Displaying Data: Bar Graph *(cont.)*

This assignment depends on the information displayed in the data table for marble fall times on the previous page.

Using the average value of marble fall times for each brand of shampoo, prepare a bar graph to display the data gathered in the project. Be sure to write a title and label both the vertical and horizontal sides of the graph. Provide a key if needed. Then determine the length, width, and spacing of the bars on the grid (you may use color if you wish). Complete the graph, remembering to be neat and accurate.

Bar Graph

(Title)

label

label

Displaying Data: Circle Graph

Jack did a selective pet inventory of his Boy Scout troop. He wanted to find out how many of the 28 Scouts owned one pet only—a cat, a dog, or a bird. His data is listed in the data table shown on this page.

1. Add and record the totals for this data table in the bottom spaces.

2. To complete this project, display this data in a circle graph on the next page. You may wish to use different colors or shadings for the different sections of your circle graph. Be sure to be neat and accurate in your display.

Data Table

Scouts Owning a Cat, a Dog, or a Bird as a Pet

Pet	Number of Scouts Owning Pets	Percent (%)
Cat	14	50%
Dog	7	25%
Bird	7	25%
Total		

Displaying Data: Circle Graph *(cont.)*

Prepare a circle graph to display Jack's results shown in the data table on page 109. Be sure to include a title and labels.

Circle Graph

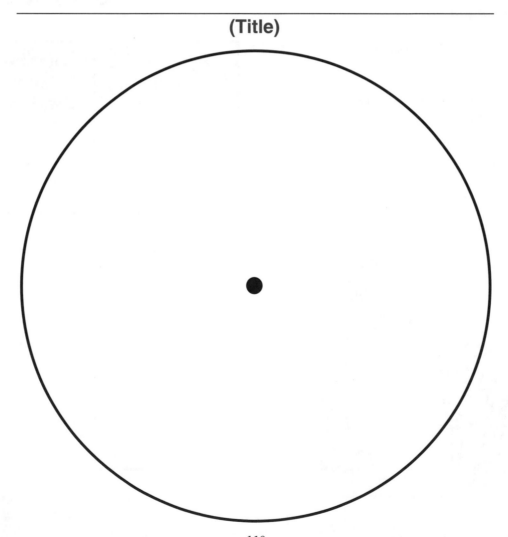

(Title)

Interpreting Data to Draw a Conclusion

Write a conclusion statement for the following project. First, carefully read the hypothesis and pay close attention to the results. In your conclusion, indicate whether the hypothesis is supported or not supported.

1. First Project

Hypothesis

Brand A Toothpaste whitens teeth better than Brand B Toothpaste .

Results

- Teeth brushed three times a day for three weeks with Brand B Toothpaste became whiter.

- Teeth brushed three times a day for three weeks with Brand A Toothpaste did not change in color.

Conclusion

_____

_____

_____

_____

_____

_____

_____

_____

_____

_____

_____

_____

_____

Interpreting Data to Draw a Conclusion *(cont.)*

Carefully read the second project (below) and pay close attention to the results. In your conclusion, indicate whether the hypothesis is supported or not supported.

2. **Second Project**

Hypothesis

Tea will prolong the life of cut flowers.

Results

- Cut flowers in water without tea began to wither after three days.

- Cut flowers in water containing tea began to wither after six days.

Conclusion

_____

_____

_____

_____

_____

_____

_____

_____

_____

_____

_____

_____

_____

Displaying the Project

Writing the Science Project Report

After scientists complete research projects, they usually make the results available to the public. They prepare **research reports** and papers that are published in scholarly journals such as the *Journal of Chemical Education*.

You also need to make their research activities and results available to the public. The best way to do this is to use your science project journals to prepare a written report about your science project. These reports will become part of the science fair project displays.

Look over your report and, if necessary, ask others and your teacher to make suggestions for improvement. Get your teacher's approval for the report before it becomes part of the science fair project display.

Be sure that your report includes the following sections:

Project Report

- ❏ Project Title
- ❏ Student's Name
- ❏ Date
- ❏ Question
- ❏ Hypothesis
- ❏ Materials Needed
- ❏ Procedure
- ❏ Results
- ❏ Conclusion
- ❏ References

Preparing a Display Board

The project **display board** is an important part of each display. It catches the viewer's attention and explains what was done and what was learned in the investigation. In addition to the information contained in the science project report, the board may include **charts**, **tables**, **graphs**, **photographs**, and other **illustrations**.

Be aware that each display looks more interesting if it has a catchy title. The title is the first thing that people see when they look at a display. For a project about the different ways rocks fall, for example, a catchy title might be "Falling Rocks." Curious people will want to find out more about this project.

Try to plan ahead. It helps to draw diagrams to show the layout of your displays. Also, you should prepare a list of materials needed for your displays.

Ask your teacher for assistance in selecting and obtaining materials needed for your displays. You may want to use items like string, construction paper, cardboard, metallic paper, poster board, foil, and cloth.

Preparing a Display Board *(cont.)*

It is usually best to do the lettering for the various sections of your display on separate pieces of paper. You may use rulers and pens or computer software packages such as *Word Perfect* to make your titles and section headings. Remember to use very large letters for the display title.

Don't forget to refer to your display diagrams and lists of needed display materials when assembling your display. Remember to put up background materials first. Then you should arrange things on individual panels or boards before securing them with tape and glue. Also, make sure you allow room for titles and other lettering.

It is a good idea to write your name on important display items. If they should get misplaced or moved during the fair exhibit, you will be able to identify them if you have labeled them with your name. Ask your teacher to check and approve your display.

Using a Multimedia Approach

Materials and Equipment

In order to increase interest and further explain what was done in an investigation, it is a good idea to place important materials and equipment in front of the display board. For example, you can display models used in their investigations. These can be three-dimensional objects that viewers can pick up to examine. A project on the aerodynamic design of various airplanes could include models of these planes in the display. Anyone wishing to do so could examine how the different airplanes are constructed.

Demonstrations

In addition to placing important materials and equipment in front of a display board, you can actually use these materials to perform demonstrations for viewers. These not only attract interest but also help explain exactly how an experiment was conducted. A project about producing colors, for example, might include demonstrations where food colors are mixed together. Nothing can stimulate interest in a project quite so effectively as an actual demonstration. Think of stores where crowds gather to watch a vendor demonstrate a special vegetable "slicer and dicer" or a new type of power tool. If you have ever seen this sort of thing, you will know that demonstrations can be very effective. Of course, it is important to practice your demonstration in advance. You will want to perform it without mistakes or accidents.

Using a Multimedia Approach *(cont.)*

Multimedia

One way of defining **multimedia** is to say that it means "many ways." The more ways you use to show something, the better people will understand and appreciate it. What this means to students is that science displays can be enhanced by using a multimedia approach. Such an approach allows one to communicate information in a variety of ways. It includes written materials like books, audio materials such as CDs and cassettes, and visual materials such as videos and computers. Discuss these items with your classmates and teacher and try to incorporate one or more into your science project displays.

Written Materials

Written materials such as books and guides provide additional information to those who view a project. Displaying a minerals guide, for example, complements a project on rocks and minerals.

Another suggestion is to provide written material to give to viewers. For example, the project investigator for rocks and minerals might print some extra copies of the steps needed for anyone to test mineral hardness. Give them away and invite others to try the tests themselves on rocks at home.

MINERALS GUIDE

MOHS HARDNESS SCALE
1 TALC
2 GYPSUM
3 CALCITE
4 FLOURITE
5 APATITE
6 ORTHOCLASE
7 QUARTZ
8 TOPAZ
9 CORUNDUM
10 DIAMOND

Using a Multimedia Approach *(cont.)*

Audio Materials

Used to provide background music, CDs can set the tone and atmosphere of a science display. It's fun to see if you can select the type of music that best represents your project. Would you choose rock music for your project on rocks and minerals, for example? Would you choose slow, soft music for a project connected to the rain forest? Your choice (whether lighthearted or serious) can mean a big boost for your display. (Don't forget that users of CDs need CD players and electrical outlets available at their display setup locations.)

Cassettes, in some instances, can highly improve a science display. Consider studies about birdcalls and animal sounds. Playing tapes with these sounds sets the stage and provides additional information and excitement. In fact, if you provide a chart with pictures of the birds, you can ask viewers to see if they can match the calls to the correct birds. In that way, you are able to actively involve the audience in your project. (Don't forget that users of cassettes require tape players and outlets available at their display setup locations.)

Visual Materials

Videos shown at a display will allow people to see your investigation in progress. Suppose that you are going to carry out a science project comparing different types of tires on remote control cars. The cars could be videotaped as you have them compete in races on a large track and on an obstacle course. Later, the races and their excitement and results could be shared with others on video. Such things as variables (the tires) and controls (the cars and tracks) could be shown in closeup views and explained as the investigation proceeded. A video record of this sort of investigation also lets the person who carried out the project go back over the work to see if any steps have been left out or might be improved. What seems like a good idea for a display may turn out to be a good idea for the entire project. (Again, don't forget that users of videos need monitors, VCRs, and electrical outlets available at their display setup locations.)

Using a Multimedia Approach *(cont.)*

Visual Materials *(cont.)*

Computers add technology and special effects to a science display. They can be used to make calculations, to display data, and to provide simulations. A simulation is a type of imitation. Suppose you are considering a science project on the movement of ocean waves. Providing actual wave movements or models for display might be next to impossible. A computer simulation on wave motion, however, could provide a colorful, moving imitation of ocean waves. Also, graphs, charts, and tables can be projected in easy-to-see color. Such visual technology really helps viewers understand your project. (Remember that computer setups need monitors, hard drives, keyboards, and electrical outlets available at their display locations. They may also need specific computer software packages and programs.)

A good procedure is for students to brainstorm in class to come up with ideas and ways to incorporate the multimedia approach into their displays. Ask your teacher to provide you with assistance and encouragement. Remember that the students making tapes will need blank tapes and access to tape recorders, and those preparing videos will need blank videocassettes and the use of a video camera.

Try to obtain the necessary equipment setup assistance you need. Perhaps you can ask the audiovisual technician at the school to visit and give a special presentation to the class.

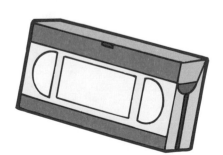

Giving an Oral Presentation

To prepare for an oral presentation, students should first write brief outlines about their science projects. The outlines should include the following sections:

1. **Heading** (name, grade, school, and project title)
2. **Question**
3. **Hypothesis**
4. **Materials**
5. **Procedure**
6. **Results**
7. **Conclusion**
8. **References**

Each outline section should be described in one or two sentences. You should practice your oral presentations at home. Sometimes it's a good idea to stand in front of a mirror. During the presentation, try to relax and look at the audience. Also, speak clearly and show enthusiasm for the project.

For practice and to build confidence, everyone might give an oral presentation of a science project to the class. Also, be sure to allow time for questions and answers.

Speaking Tips

❑ Speak clearly and slowly. (Nervousness tends to make us speak more rapidly.)

❑ Look to the left side of the room for a sentence or two and then turn to the right side to address the other people.

❑ Until you build up the confidence to look right at individuals in the audience, it helps to focus your eyes just above their heads.

❑ Hold up visual aids—materials, charts, and models—so that all can see. Use as many of these as seems practical. This practice makes the speaker feel more at ease because the audience attention is then on the display and not on the speaker.

❑ Use a pointer to call attention to diagrams.

❑ Sometimes you can use a helper to hold up a display while you point out important illustrations or parts.

The Science Project Report

Use the following science project report form as a guide for writing about your science fair investigation. Be sure to include all the sections. When you finish, show it to your teacher for approval.

Project Title: _____

_____

Student's Name:_____

Date: _____

Question

_____

_____

Hypothesis

_____

_____

_____

Materials Needed

_____

_____

_____

_____

_____

_____

_____

/ _____

_____

_____

The Science Project Report *(cont.)*

Procedure (step-by-step directions)

_____

_____

_____

_____

_____

Conclusion

_____

_____

_____

_____

_____

_____

Results

_____

_____

_____

_____

_____

References

_____

_____

_____

_____

_____

Project Display Board

Diagram of Project Display

Plan your science fair project display in advance.

Organize where you will place each title, the charts, information, diagrams, etc.

Draw a few diagrams and choose the layout that you think *best* represents your project.

Project Display Board *(cont.)*

Materials Needed for the Display

Prepare a list of materials needed for your display.

If possible, use your materials to perform demonstrations for viewers.

Place important materials and equipment in front of the display board.

A Multimedia Approach

Remember that you can improve science project displays by placing additional materials and equipment in front of the display board. These items can make a display look more interesting and further explain the investigation. They include books, equipment, models, and demonstrations.

Using a multimedia approach adds variety to a display. It includes written materials such as books and printed handouts, audio materials like CDs and cassettes, and visual materials such as videos and computers.

Brainstorming

Brainstorm with others about your science project display. Decide whether any of the categories on the following pages can be used in the display. If so, describe the uses in the space provided. You may want to ask your teacher for assistance.

A Multimedia Approach *(cont.)*

Brainstorming *(cont.)*

Books and Printed Material

_____

_____

_____

_____

_____

Equipment

_____

_____

_____

Models

_____

_____

Demonstrations

_____

_____

_____

_____

CDs

_____

_____

_____

A Multimedia Approach *(cont.)*

Brainstorming *(cont.)*

Cassettes

_____

_____

_____

_____

_____

Computers

_____

_____

_____

_____

_____

Videos

_____

_____

_____

_____

Other

_____

_____

_____

_____

The Oral Presentation

Complete the following outline to prepare a guide for your oral presentation.

Heading

My name is _____. I am in

the _____ grade and attend _____

_____ school.

My project title is _____ .

Question

My science project question was _____

_____

_____

_____

_____?

Hypothesis

My hypothesis was _____

_____

_____ .

Materials

The materials used in my investigation included the following:

_____

_____

_____

_____

_____

The Oral Presentation *(cont.)*

Complete the following outline to add to page 129 as a guide for your oral presentation.

Procedure

I tested my hypothesis by _____

_____

_____

_____ .

Results

The results of my investigation were _____

_____

_____

_____ .

Conclusion

Based on my experimental results, I concluded that

(Mention whether your hypothesis was supported.)

_____

_____

_____ .

References

References I used were the following:

_____

_____

_____

_____

Practice Projects

Testing Towels

(Science Investigation: *osmosis and capillary action*)

Rapid Rising

Problem: Which brand of paper towel (A, B, C, or D) will absorb (soak up) water the fastest?

Hypothesis: Brand _____ will absorb water the fastest.

Materials: four different brands of paper towels, water, clear plastic cups, food coloring, spoon, timing device with seconds

Variables: four different brands of towels

Controls: The controls in this experiment are the amount of water, food coloring, and starting time.

Procedure

1. Fill a clear plastic cup almost full of water. Place a few drops of food coloring in the water and stir.

2. Carefully tear four paper towels from four different brands of paper towel along the perforated lines.

3. Roll each towel into a long, thin tube about equal in length to each other.

4. Mark the name of each towel on one end of the tube.

5. Write down the exact time. Place all four tubes in the cup at the same time.

6. Observe how the colored water climbs the paper towel tubes.

7. Keep track of which towel the water climbs fastest, reaching the end of the tube, and which is second, third, and fourth.

8. Keep track of the elapsed times for each.

9. Using fresh towels (of the same brands) each time, do two more trials to confirm your results.

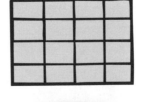

Testing Towels *(cont.)*

Rapid Rising *(cont.)*

Data: Make a data chart recording your results. Make a bar graph using the average times from three trials to illustrate your data chart.

Data Chart: **Towel Speed of Absorption**

Brand	Time			
	Trial 1	Trial 2	Trial 3	Average
A				
B				
C				
D				

Results: _____

_____

Bar Graph: **Towel Speed of Absorption**

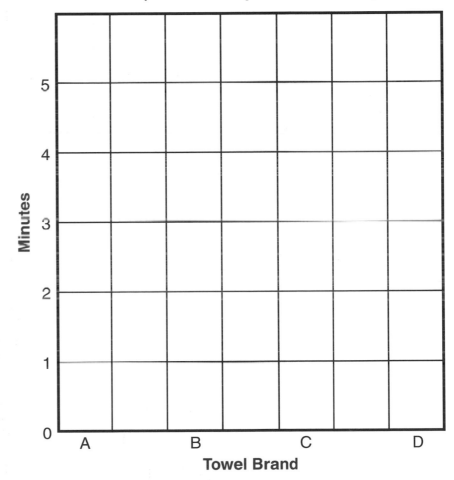

Conclusion: (Was your hypothesis supported or not supported?) _____

_____

Testing Towels *(cont.)*

Squeeze Play

Problem: Which brand of paper towel will absorb the greatest amount of water?

Hypothesis: Brand _____ will absorb the greatest amount of water.

Materials: four different brands of paper towels, water, clear plastic cups, measuring cup (graduated in milliliters or cubic centimeters, if possible)

Variables: The variables are the four different brands of paper towels.

Controls: The controls are the water and the time used for each towel.

Procedure

1. Arrange the four paper towel tubes as was described in Rapid Rising (page 132). Make sure that only one piece of toweling is used from each brand and that they are about the same size, torn along the perforation as you would do in taking a paper towel for use. Make sure you have marked the brand name on each towel.

2. Wait until all four towels have absorbed water and are dripping onto the table.

3. Carefully remove one towel. Record the brand name.

4. Gently squeeze every drop from the towel into an empty, clear plastic cup.

5. Pour the squeezed water into a measuring cup to determine exactly how many milliliters (or cubic centimeters) of water it holds. If your measuring cup does not indicate milliliters or cubic centimeters, you can use fractions of a fluid ounce on the cup or millimeters measurement on a ruler to measure the height of the water.

6. Squeeze the water out of each towel in turn and record the amount of water the paper towel held.

7. Using fresh towels for each brand, record two more trials to confirm your results.

Testing Towels *(cont.)*

Squeeze Play *(cont.)*

Data: Make a data chart recording the amount of water absorbed by each towel for each trial and then figure the average amounts.

Brand	Amount Absorbed			
	Trial 1	Trial 2	Trial 3	Average
A				
B				
C				
D				

Results: Make a bar graph from your data chart, illustrating your results. Depending on which measurement you used, label amounts as milliliters, cubic centimeters, or ounces.

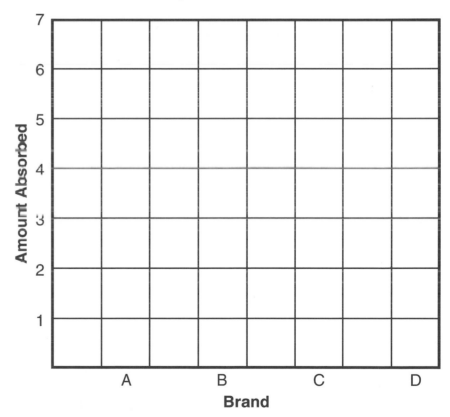

Conclusions: (Was your hypothesis supported or not supported?) _____

_____

Testing Towels (cont.)

Sipping Siphons

Problem: Exactly how do siphons work? Can they suck all the water out of one container into another?

Hypothesis: (Supply your own words here.)_____

_____

Materials: four different brands of paper towels, water, clear plastic cups, food coloring

Variables: The variables are the different brands of paper towels.

Controls: The controls are the same water supply and cups of the same size.

Procedure

1. Choose any two of your paper towel brands.

2. Position two empty, clear plastic cups on either side of a full cup of colored water.

3. Roll one towel from each brand into a long, thin tube. Bend the tubes slightly and put both of them into the cup of colored water. Write down the exact time.

4. As the water climbs up the paper towels, bend each tube so that it is leaning over one of the empty plastic cups.

5. Record the name of the towel leaning over each empty cup.

6. Leave the cups and paper towels undisturbed.

Testing Towels *(cont.)*

Sipping Siphons *(cont.)*

7. Observe what happens to the water that has climbed up the paper towels.

   ☐ Did the paper towels fill each cup as high as the water remaining in the first cup?

   ☐ Which paper towel carried water faster than the other?

   ☐ Repeat this activity but place the full cup of colored water on a book or some elevated position with the empty cups at a lower level.

   ☐ How much water is carried out of the first cup?

   ☐ Did either of the two empty cups fill more than the other?

   ☐ Repeat the activity with the empty cups situated on a book or raised area and the full cup at a lower level.

   ☐ Describe what happens to the water.

   ☐ Determine which paper towel holds the most water.

   ☐ Would this indicate it is the best towel? Why?

Data: Decide how to measure your data and put it into data chart.

Results: Can you draw a diagram to show your results from the data chart? Try it.

Conclusions: (Was your hypothesis supported? Did you learn something not even considered in your hypothesis? If so, write down what you did learn.)

Testing Towels (cont.)

The Dry Test

The Problem: How can you test the strength of a dry paper towel?

Hypothesis: You can test the strength of a dry paper towel by adding weights to it until it tears.

Materials: four different brands of paper towels, masking tape, a large supply of pennies

Variables: paper towel brand

Controls: pennies, tape, desk

Procedure

1. Use four pieces of masking tape to attach the four corners of one dry paper towel to an area between two desks.

2. Allow about two inches (5 cm) of each side of the towel to lie on the desk. The rest of the towel will be between the desks.

3. Keep count as you place pennies on the stretched-out paper towel.

4. Place as many pennies on the dry towel as you can until it breaks or tears apart. Retest to observe if the tape alone gives way.

5. Test each of your four paper towel brands in the same way. (Can you put more than 100 pennies on any one towel?)

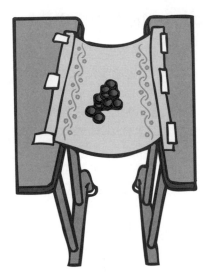

Data: Make a data chart recording your findings.

Results: Make a bar graph showing how many pennies each of your paper towels held.

More Investigation: Design another way of testing the strength of paper towels. (Hint: How much can you lift with your paper towels?)

The Wet Test

- Try the same tests after dipping a paper towel in water and gently squeezing out any excess water.

- Keep an accurate count of your results and make a chart and graph for the wet trials. (Can you get more than 50 pennies on any wet towel? Did any of your towels do as well or better when wet?)

Testing Towels *(cont.)*

Double-Layer Towels

Do two layers of towels actually work much better than one layer? Repeat the dry paper towel test that you used on page 138, using two layers of paper towel for the test.

Tape the first layer of towel and then the second layer. Record how many pennies the double layer holds for each brand. Do you get more than 150 pennies on any one double towel layer? Which results surprise you? Why?

Test the strength of double layers of wet paper towels in the same way. Tape each layer separately and gradually place pennies on the stretched-out layers.

- Are any of the double layers particularly strong?
- Can you get more than 75 pennies on any wet double layer?
- Do any of the results surprise you?

The Stretch Test

How far will each paper towel stretch before it tears? Test one layer of each brand of dry paper towel in this manner:

1. Fold one paper towel lengthwise into four layers.

2. Hold one end of the paper towel near the beginning of a ruler and pull gently on the other end until the paper towel tears apart.

3. Record how far each brand of paper towel stretched beyond its original length before breaking.

Test the stretching capacity of the four brands of paper towels when they are wet.

1. Soak each paper towel. Wring out excess water.

2. Lay the wet towel along the length of the ruler and record how far it will stretch before tearing.

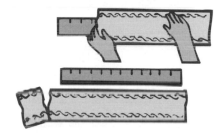

Design Your Own Tests

Since paper towels are used for many things, try designing some of your own tests to determine the best brand.

Possibilities: strength tests with soapy water, ability to soak up cooking oil, strength tests to hold different objects, number of towels needed to clean up a specific spill

Rocket, Rocket

(Science Investigation: *propulsion and trajectory*)

Balloon Blast-Off

Problem: How well do balloons work as rockets? Will some shapes work better than others?

Hypothesis: Balloons will make good rockets. The largest balloon will work the best, no matter what shape it is.

Materials: balloons of several shapes and sizes, index cards, ruler, markers, crayons, tape, fishing line, vinegar, baking soda, tissue paper, corks, small clear plastic bottles, straws

Variables: different shapes and sizes of balloons

Controls: same size rocket model to tape to the balloons

Procedure

1. Use an index card or tagboard to make a rocket like the one shown.

2. Color the rocket pattern and roll it into a cylinder. Tape the cylinder in place.

3. Blow up a balloon and hold it in the inflated condition as a partner gently tapes the rocket model to the top or side of the balloon.

4. Take the balloon rocket to the designated launch area inside or outside the classroom.

5. Set the balloon rocket on the launching pad, lean away from the rocket, and release the balloon.

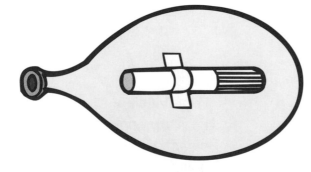

Rocket, Rocket (cont.)

Balloon Blast-Off (cont.)

- How well did your rocket work?

- Try launching the rocket again with a different balloon. Try long balloons, twisties, large spherical balloons, and any other sizes and shapes available.

6. Try the slender rocket design shown on this page. This design curves into a long slender tube. It can be attached to the top or side of the balloon.

7. With which balloon did this design work best?

8. Design your own rocket version. Modify one of the two designs already shown or create an entirely new design.

9. Try launching your new design, using a long, slender type of balloon.

Data: Make a data chart showing which type of balloon and which type of rocket design went the farthest.

Conclusions: Did the long, slender design and balloon work best? If so, why do you think this might be?

Rocket, Rocket (cont.)

Beeline Balloons

You can often get greater distance by guiding your balloon—that is, making it fly on a beeline!

Procedure

1. Cut a 30-foot (9-meter) piece of monofilament fishing line. Tie one end to the shaft of a pushpin and pin that end to a bulletin board about four feet (1.2 m) off the floor or to a tree or pole outdoors.

2. Extend the string across the room or playground to the farthest distance possible. Keep the fishing line out of the path of students and tape it against a wall until you are ready to launch.

3. Copy the design shown on this page onto an index card, manila folder, or similar thick paper. Color it with markers or crayons and cut it out.

4. Tape the rocket design onto a straw in two places.

5. Thread the end of the fishing line through the straw and hold it in place while a partner blows up a balloon and tapes it onto the rocket model.

6. Hold the string and model so that the straw sits easily on the fishing line and the fishing line is aimed slightly higher than where it is pinned.

7. Release the balloon and observe how well the rocket travels. Did it get to the end of the fishing line?

   - Did the straw catch or run freely along the fishing line? Did the balloon seem to run out of air before the rocket reached the end of the line?

   - Do several trials of your rocket. Use balloons of different styles and sizes. Hold the fishing line at different angles to get the maximum degree of speed.

   - Create a model rocket of your own. Use a different style or type of rocket. Make your rocket longer or shorter, wider or narrower.

   - Try several different versions. Use different balloons and test each of your models.

   - Try mounting your rocket onto a double-length straw (two straws that you have hooked together).

   - Try making a cylinder to go around the straw.

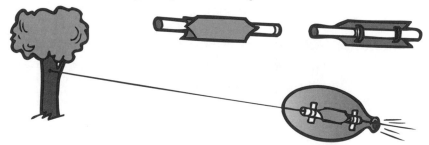

Rocket, Rocket *(cont.)*

Kitchen Chemicals

Problem: Can you make a rocket from kitchen chemicals? How do you do it? How far can such a rocket propel an object?

Hypothesis: Vinegar and baking soda will create carbon dioxide gas, which can be used to propel an object if the gas is safely enclosed and then released.

Materials: facial tissue; baking soda; vinegar; measuring cup; small, clear plastic bottle; cork to fit the plastic bottle; fishing line; straws; aluminum foil; masking tape; paper

Variables: amounts of vinegar and baking soda

Controls: size of bottle, cork, and "astronaut"

Procedure

1. Lay a facial tissue flat on the desk. Carefully use the measuring cup to pour 25 cc of baking soda in a row down the middle of the tissue. Make sure the baking soda is spread evenly along the row.

2. Carefully fold the tissue into a long, thin tube with no areas where the baking soda is bunched up.

3. Cut four pieces of fishing line, each about four inches (10 cm) long.

4. Tie one piece of fishing line at one end and one at the other end of the tube.

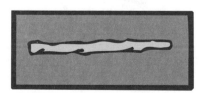

Rocket, Rocket *(cont.)*

Kitchen Chemicals *(cont.)*

Procedure *(cont.)*

5. Tie the other two pieces along the length of the tube so that the baking soda can't bunch very much at any point along the tube.

6. Carefully fit a cork into the mouth of the empty bottle. Wine corks or craft store corks are both acceptable. Cover the shaft of the cork with two layers of masking tape. This will help prevent any gas from escaping from the pores in the cork and will make it fit tighter in the mouth of the bottle.

7. Make a miniature astronaut from a small piece of straw, aluminum foil, and paper as shown. Tape the astronaut to the top of the cork.

8. Pour six ounces (177 mL) of vinegar into the clear plastic bottle and take all your materials outdoors to the designated launch area.

9. When you are ready to launch, slip the tube of baking soda into the bottle and immediately fit the cork tightly into the bottle opening.

10. Carefully and firmly hold the bottle pointing away from yourself and others and give it several hard shakes. The carbon dioxide gas should propel the cork and astronaut several yards up into the air.

Rocket, Rocket *(cont.)*

Lift-Off Launchers

Procedure

1. Make a small cone of aluminum foil to fit on the cork instead of the astronaut.

2. Measure an area on the playground that can be used for a launch site. Use chalk or a marker to indicate a starting line and distances of five feet (1.5 m), 10 feet (3 m), and so forth up to 75 feet (23 m).

3. Clean your bottle and make a new tube of baking soda as you did before. Pour six ounces (177 mL) of fresh vinegar into the bottle.

4. When you are ready to launch, stand at the starting line, slip your baking soda tube into the bottle, and fit the cork with the cone tightly into the bottle.

5. Point the bottle down the marked launching area, hold it tightly, and shake it vigorously. **Never point the bottle at anyone.**

6. When your rocket has been launched, retrieve your cork and cone and note how far it traveled.

   - Did the tube stay in the bottle or fly out?

   - Why do you think some rockets travel farther than others?

   - Try a new version. Try using fewer ounces of vinegar and even less baking soda.

   - Redesign your cone to make it more streamlined, longer, or different in some way.

7. Use a larger bottle to design a rocket that you can shake and set on a launching pad before it goes off. **Do not use more than six ounces (170) ml of vinegar!** Use different types of tubes, tissues of various types, and change other variables to create rockets of your own design.

Data: Create a data table to record your results.

Conclusion: What did you discover?

Remember the following safety rules:

- Always point a rocket away from yourself and others.

- Hold the rocket firmly.

- Use the rocket only in a designated area and **never** indoors!

Parachute Packages

(Science Investigation: *air resistance and air taking up space*)

Simple Chutes

Problem: How do parachutes work? Are some better than others? Why?

Hypothesis: The air pushes against the parachute like a sail, slowing down the fall. Big ones should be better than small ones.

Materials: fishing line, paper, newspaper, small plastic trash bags, large trash bags, construction paper, large paper clips, manila folder or tagboard, plastic bottles, boxes, hole punch or pushpin, masking tape, scissors

Variables: size and material of parachutes and weights

Controls: height from which different parachutes are dropped

Procedure

1. Fold an 8½" x 11" (22 cm x 28 cm) piece of paper in fourths.

2. Unfold the paper so that all four folds face up.

3. Cover each corner on both sides with a piece of masking tape.

4. Use a hole punch or pushpin to make a hole at all four corners. Make the hole right through the tape.

5. Cut four pieces of fishing line, each about 16" (40 cm) long.

6. Tie one piece of fishing line at each corner.

7. Tape three large paper clips together. Draw a small figure of a parachutist to tape onto the paper clips.

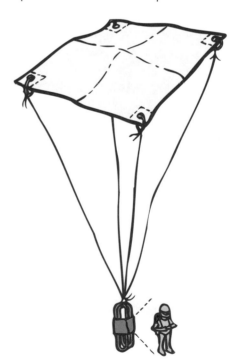

Parachute Packages *(cont.)*

Simple Chutes *(cont.)*

Procedure *(cont.)*

8. Tie all four ends of the fishing line together an even distance from the corners. Tie or tape them to the paper-clip parachutist.

9. Hold your parachute as high as you can by the chute or canopy and drop it. Note how fast it falls and whether the canopy slows the fall.

10. Stand on a chair, stage, or stairs, if available, and drop the parachute from a higher level.

11. Try folding the entire chute and throwing it high into the air. Does it unfold in time or fall too soon?

12. Try using different paper in your parachute. Try a different thickness or overlapping two pieces of paper.

13. Make a new parachutist. It might be heavier or lighter. You can try using other materials such as pencils, scissors, erasers, a ruler, or a wad of paper.

14. Try folding the canopy different ways. You might try to have eight folds rather than four folds.

Data: Prepare a data chart to show your trial results.

Conclusions: Which parachute turned out to be the best?

Why? _____

_____

_____

_____

_____

_____

_____

_____

Parachute Packages *(cont.)*

Heavier Chutes

Problem: See page 146.

Hypothesis: See page 146.

Variables: See page 146.

Controls: See page 146.

Materials: See page 146.

Procedure

Use a large piece of construction paper to make a heavier and stronger canopy.

1. Make a two-inch (5-cm) fold along the narrower edge. Keep folding the paper over until you have folded the entire piece. Every fold will face the same way.

2. Fold the paper once in half lengthwise.

3. Place a piece of tape on both sides of all four corners for reinforcement.

4. Use the hole punch or pushpin to make a hole in each corner right through the taped corners.

5. Cut four pieces of fishing line two feet (.6 m) long.

6. Tie one piece of fishing line at each corner.

7. Tape six large paper clips together. Draw a small figure of a parachutist to tape onto the paper clips.

8. Tie all four ends of the fishing line together an even distance from the corners. Then tie or tape them to the paper-clip parachutist.

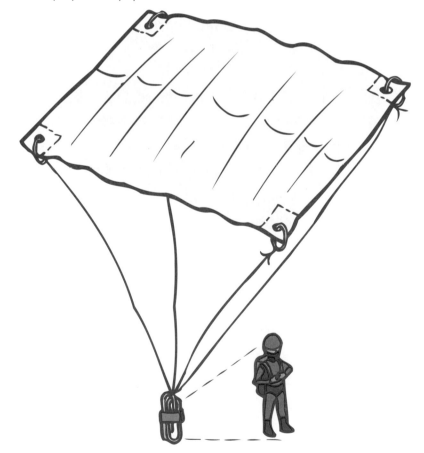

Parachute Packages (cont.)

Newspaper Canopies

Problem: See page 146.

Hypothesis: See page 146.

Materials: See page 146.

Variables: See page 146.

Controls: See page 146.

Procedure

1. Fold a newspaper in half to make a canopy about the size of the construction paper. Fold the narrower side over two inches (5 cm) and continue folding over as you did with the construction paper. Fold the newspaper once in half the long way.

2. Tape all four corners so that the two pieces of newspaper are connected and to reinforce the corners.

3. Use the hole punch or pushpin to make a hole in each corner right through the tape. Cut four pieces of fishing line two feet (.6 m) long and tie them to each corner as you did before.

4. Attach the six-paper-clip parachutist you used before or make a new one.

5. Test this model and the construction paper model on page 148 from various heights, comparing your results with your previous trials.

Data: Add your data to the data chart begun with the other parachute tests.

Conclusions

See if you can describe the actions of each different chute clearly. Other people should be able to tell which one (or ones) you thought was the best. Can you explain why one (or more) seemed to do better than the others? Was size the only difference, or did different materials and design change performance?

Parachute Packages *(cont.)*

Plastic Canopies

Problem: See page 146.

Hypothesis: See page 146.

Materials: See page 146.

Variables: See page 146.

Controls: See page 146.

Procedure

1. Use a small plastic trash bag to make the canopy. Leave the bag unopened but spread out on the desk. Place a piece of masking tape on both sides of all four corners for reinforcement.

2. Make a hole in each taped corner. Cut four pieces of fishing line two feet (.6 m) long for each corner. Attach the fishing line to the corners.

3. Use a small plastic bottle for the parachutist. Draw a figure of a parachutist to tape onto the bottle.

4. Tie all four ends of the fishing line together an even distance from the corners and then tie or tape them to the bottle. Test this model by dropping it from a high elevation.

5. Try wrapping the chute around the bottle and throwing it high into the air. Do several trials. Did it open and slow the fall of the bottle?

6. Put an ounce (30 mL) of water in the bottle and cap it. Try dropping and throwing the chute again. Did it slow the bottle? How much water can you put into the bottle before the parachute "flames out" and won't open?

Parachute Packages *(cont.)*

Multilayered Canopies

Procedure

1. Use either newspaper or plastic trash bags to make a double-layered canopy. Make the parachute as you have made others with the newspaper or plastic bag. Use fishing line two feet (.6 m) long or longer.

2. Two inches (5 cm) below the first canopy, run the fishing line through a hole in each corner of the second canopy and tie or tape it in place.

3. Test this version and compare results with your earlier models.

Dropping Heavier Objects

Procedure

1. Pack a small, shoebox-sized box with packing material and an egg (or some other inexpensive but delicate object).

2. Design a parachute to protect the egg box when it is dropped off a one-story roof or staircase.

3. You may want to modify the design of the parachute made from a large plastic trash bag. You can slit open this large bag and use the four corners to make a very large canopy for your parachute.

4. You will need to securely tape or tie the chute to the box and do a few practice trials without the egg to determine how well the parachute will work with the box.

   • Did your parachute protect the egg?

   • What could you do to improve the parachute design?

Data: Create a data chart for your last two trials.

Conclusions: Clearly describe your results so that others can understand which designs performed the best.

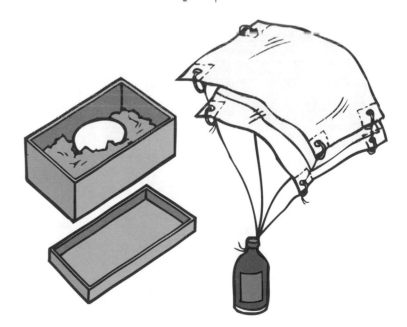

Pendulum Power

(Science Investigation: *how pendulums work*)

A Simple Pendulum

Problem: How does a pendulum work?

Hypothesis: A weight at the end of a line causes the line to keep moving once it has been started.

Materials: fishing line, large paper clips, tape, wood doweling or rod, ruler

Variables: height at which the bob is released, size of weight or bob, and length of the line

Controls: size of weight or bob and length of the line

Procedure

1. For a hanger, use wood doweling that is about two feet (.6 Δ102m) long. (You may use an inexpensive bamboo garden stake or any other stick in place of a dowel.)

2. Tape the hanger between two desks of the same height about 18 inches (46 cm) apart.

3. Cut a piece of fishing line about 16 inches (40 cm) long. Tie one end of the line securely to the hanger.

4. Use a ruler to measure one foot (30 cm) down from the hanger.

5. Tape three large paper clips together to form the bob of the pendulum. (You can use two metal washers instead, if you wish.)

6. Tie the bob to the end of the line one foot (30 cm) from the hanger.

Pendulum Power *(cont.)*

A Simple Pendulum *(cont.)*

Procedure *(cont.)*

7. Hold the bob the length of the fishing line and even with the level of the hanger and desks.

8. Release the bob and time how long it takes to hang motionless again.

9. Hold the bob the length of the fishing line again and even with the level of the hangers and desks.

10. Release the bob and count the number of swings the pendulum makes before it hangs motionless again. Count one forward and one backward movement as one complete cycle.

11. Hold the bob above the level of the hanger and release it so that it swings evenly without jerking.

12. Try several angles above the hanger level.

    - How high can you hold it and still get an even—not jerky—swing?

    - Can you hold it directly above the hanger and get a smooth swing?

    - Does the pendulum swing longer if it is released from a higher angle?

    - At what angle do you get the longest period of swinging?

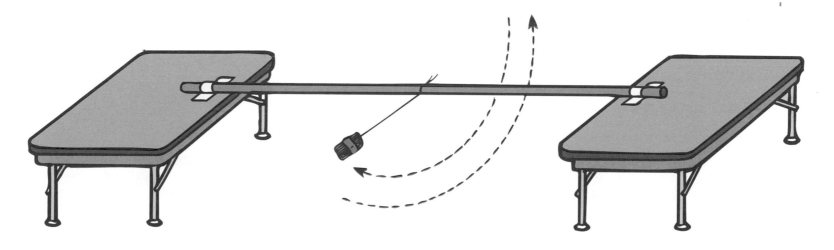

Pendulum Power *(cont.)*

Bob Weight

Procedure

1. Move the desks as far apart as you can and still securely hold the hanger between them.

2. Move the pendulum you have been using.

3. Tape six large paper clips together to form a bob twice as heavy as the one you have been using.

4. Cut another piece of fishing line about 16 inches (40 cm) long and suspend the bob on this pendulum exactly the same length as the other one. Adjust the fishing line until you are certain they are an even length.

5. Adjust the two pendulums on the hanger until they are far enough apart so as not to swing into each other or to swing into the sides of the desks.

6. Hold the two bobs at their full lengths, even with the level of the hanger and the desks.

7. Release the bobs at the same time.

8. Observe the speeds of the bobs and how they swing.

9. Do at least three trials of the bobs.

   - Do they swing at the same rhythm?

   - Do you think the weight of the bob affects its swing?

Heavyweight Bobs

Procedure

1. Add three more large paper clips to the bob with six paper clips.

2. Tape them securely. Make sure they are exactly the same length as the three-clip bob.

3. Again, hold the two bobs at their full length even with the level of the hanger and the desks.

4. Release the bobs at the same time.

5. Observe the speed of the bobs and how they swing.

6. If they get tangled, adjust the bobs and try again.

7. Do at least three trials of the heavyweight bob.

   - Do they swing at the same rhythm?

   - Do you think the weight of the bob affects the speed of the swing?

   - Test your opinion by making a bob with 12 large paper clips and comparing swings.

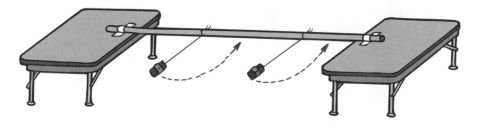

Pendulum Power *(cont.)*

Pendulum Length

Procedure

1. Remove the heavier bob. Leave the original pendulum in place.

2. Cut a piece of fishing line two feet (60 cm) long.

3. Make a three-paper-clip bob just like the original one. Tie one end of the fishing line to the bob.

4. Use a ruler to measure exactly 18 inches (46 cm) from the hanger and tie the other end of the fishing line so that this pendulum hangs exactly 18 inches (46 cm) from the hanger.

5. Arrange the two pendulums on the hanger so that they will not swing into each other or the sides of the desk.

6. Hold the two bobs at their full lengths even with the level of the hanger and the desks.

7. Release the bobs at the same time.

8. Observe the speeds of the bobs and how they swing.

9. If they get tangled, adjust the bobs and try again.

10. Do at least three trials.

- What is different about these two pendulums?

- Which pendulum always swings more slowly?

- Hold each of these bobs at the starting point. (You and a partner should each count the number of swings for each bob. Remember that one full swing back and forth counts as one cycle.)

- Which pendulum keeps swinging longer?

Longer Pendulums

Procedure

1. Move the two pendulums to one side or remove them for the moment.

2. Make one pendulum with a three-paper-clip bob that hangs only six inches (15 cm) from the hanger.

3. Make a second pendulum with a three-paper-clip bob which hangs just above the floor.

4. Hold the two pendulums level with the hanger and release them at the same time.

5. With a partner, time how long each pendulum swings until it becomes still.

6. Record your results for the data chart.

Proving Probability

(Science Investigation: *probability—the mathematical science of determining the likelihood or chance of something happening*)

Flip of the Coin

Problem: What is the likelihood (probability) of a certain side of a coin or number on dice turning up in a given trial?

Hypothesis: The chances (probability) of a certain side or number showing depend upon the total number of sides.

Materials: pennies, three dice, manila folder or tagboard, scissors, ruler, clear tape

Variables: number of trials

Controls: use of same coins and dice for each trial

Procedure

1. Number a sheet of paper from 1 to 50.

2. Flip a penny 50 times and record on your paper each time whether it lands heads or tails.

3. Count the number of heads and tails. Did you flip more heads or more tails? Was the count close?

4. Number your paper from 51 to 100 and flip the penny 50 more times. Record each head or tail flipped and compute the total number of heads and tails flipped.

5. The mathematical probability for each flip is that you have one chance in two (or a 50% chance) of flipping a head or 50 heads out of a hundred flips.

6. How many heads did you actually flip?

7. Generally, you are more likely to come close to the mathematical odds when there is a greater number of opportunities.

8. Flip the coin 100 more times. Determine how close you came to 50% (100 heads) after 200 coin flips.

9. Record each classmate's results on a chart.
   - Compute the total flips by all the students.
   - Compute and graph all the heads recorded.
   - Compute the combined percentage of heads flipped by dividing the total number of heads flipped by the total number of flips.
   - Compute the percentage of tails flipped. How close were you to 50%, a probability of one chance in two?

Proving Probability *(cont.)*

On a Roll

A cube-shaped die has six faces. The mathematical probability of rolling any specific number (such as a three) is one in six. Compare your results on this experiment with the odds.

Procedure

1. Number your paper from 1 to 48.

2. Roll the die 48 times and record which number faced up on each roll.

3. Determine how many 1s, 2s, 3s, 4s, 5s, and 6s you rolled.

The odds would indicate eight rolls for each of the numbers. Did you roll any numbers exactly eight times? Which numbers were far above or below the odds?

4. Number your paper from 49 to 96.

5. Roll the die 48 more times and record the numbers.

6. Count the total number of times each number appeared in the 96 rolls.

7. Make a chart to illustrate your results.

The mathematical odds suggest 16 rolls for each number. Did any of your numbers get rolled exactly 16 times? Were any numbers far lower or higher than the odds?

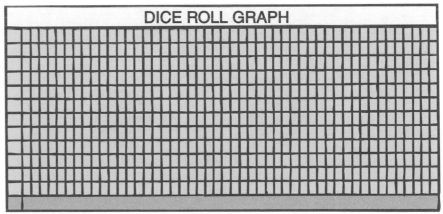

Proving Probability *(cont.)*

Two on a Roll

Procedure

1. Number your paper from 1 to 48. Roll two dice 48 times and record the total of each roll. For example, rolling a three and a two would mean a roll of five.

2. Which number between 2 and 12 was rolled most often?

3. Which other numbers were often rolled?

4. Number your paper from 49 to 96. Roll the two dice 48 more times and record each number.

5. Make a chart or graph showing the number of rolls for each number between 2 and 12.

6. Where are the most often rolled numbers located on the graph? Why do you think it is harder to roll a 12 than a 7, 8, or 9?

7. Does your graph or chart show a bulge in the center like a bell?

Three on a Roll

Procedure

1. Create a tally sheet numbered from 1 to 48.

2. Roll the three dice and record the total for each roll on the tally sheet.

3. Can you discover a pattern in the totals? (**Hint:** Try putting the numbers from the tally sheet into a graph.)

4. Which numbers seem to be the easiest to roll?

5. Roll the three dice another 48 times and record your numbers on the tally sheet. What pattern did you find?

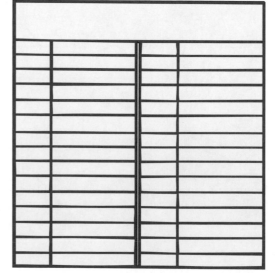

Proving Probability (cont.)

Tetrahedral Dice

Procedure

1. Cut out or copy the pattern for a tetrahedral die illustrated on this page.

2. Use tagboard or a manila folder to make the die.

3. Number the faces on the die from 1 to 4.

4. Carefully fold and tape the die with thin strips of clear tape as shown.

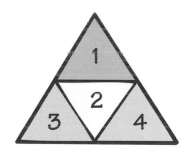

5. Roll the die 48 times and record your results on a tally sheet.

6. Use the side that lands down for this die.

7. The mathematical odds for rolling any of the four numbers would be one in four or 12 rolls per number.

8. What were your results?

Octahedral Dice

Procedure

1. Cut out or copy the pattern for an octahedral die shown on this page. Use tagboard or a manila folder to make the die. Number the faces on the die from 1 to 8.

2. Carefully fold and tape the die with thin strips of clear tape.

3. Roll the die 48 times and record your results on a tally sheet. The mathematical odds for rolling any of the eight numbers would be one in eight or six rolls per number.

4. What were your results?

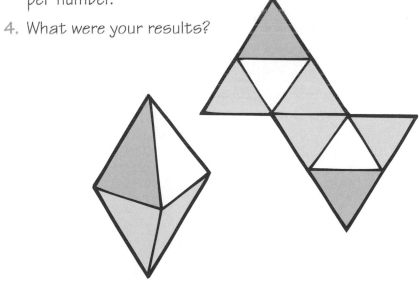

Proving Probability (cont.)

Dodecahedral Dice

Procedure

1. Make the dodecahedral die illustrated on this page as you did with the other dice on page 159. Number the faces from 1 to 12 and carefully fold and tape the die.

2. Roll this die 48 times and record the results.

3. What is the probability of rolling any one number?

4. What results did you get?

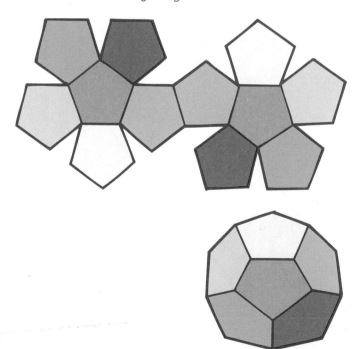

	Number Rolled											
Times Rolled	1	2	3	4	5	6	7	8	9	10	11	12
1												
2												
3												
4												
5												
6												
7												
8												
9												
10												

160